PRAISE FOR *ALL-INCLUSIVE TV*

"Hengel asked the right questions to turn TV advertising's traditional process on its head. A must-read for anyone looking for a better way to grow their business."

—Gary B. Cohen, managing partner, CO2 Partners; best-selling author of *Just Ask Leadership: Why Great Managers Always Ask the Right Questions*

"This book goes beyond brilliant marketing. Hengel calls us to step up and into taking bold action, to invest in those big moves that propel us forward and ahead of our competition. Reading these pages is like entering into a vast super-market. You'll find on each page a rich variety of quality for every leader hungry to savor the satisfying taste of scalable, profitable growth and richer organizational vitality."

—Jay Steven Levin, principal, WinThinking

"I have seen firsthand the impact that Hengel has had on emerging brands leveraging TV advertising to grow their businesses; this book is a must-read for anyone looking for a practical guide with real–world examples on how to best leverage TV advertising."

—David Horowitz, founder and CEO, Touchdown Ventures

"Chuck Hengel was one of the early pioneers of direct-response radio before entering TV. He's well known for developing innovative strategies and one-of-a-kind solutions that continue to be widely used today. Chuck is a visionary in this industry, yet highly approachable, working tire-lessly to establish Marketing Architects as one of the most respected leaders in this business."

—Colleen Szot, member of the Direct Response Hall of Fame

ALL-INCLUSIVE TV

ALL-INCLUSIVE TV

HOW BOOMING BRANDS ARE REIMAGINING TV ADVERTISING

Chuck Hengel

Published by Advantage, Charleston, South Carolina.
Member of Advantage Media Group.

ADVANTAGE is a registered trademark, and the Advantage colophon is a trademark of Advantage Media Group, Inc.

Printed in the United States of America.

10 9 8 7 6 5 4 3 2 1

ISBN: 978-1-642252-82-8
LCCN: 2021907565

Cover design by Greg Brannen.
Layout design by Megan Elger.

This publication is designed to provide accurate and authoritative information in regard to the subject matter covered. It is sold with the understanding that the publisher is not engaged in rendering legal, accounting, or other professional services. If legal advice or other expert assistance is required, the services of a competent professional person should be sought.

Advantage Media Group is proud to be a part of the Tree Neutral® program. Tree Neutral offsets the number of trees consumed in the production and printing of this book by taking proactive steps such as planting trees in direct proportion to the number of trees used to print books. To learn more about Tree Neutral, please visit **www.treeneutral.com**.

Advantage Media Group is a publisher of business, self-improvement, and professional development books and online learning. We help entrepreneurs, business leaders, and professionals share their Stories, Passion, and Knowledge to help others Learn & Grow. Do you have a manuscript or book idea that you would like us to consider for publishing? Please visit **advantagefamily.com**.

Contents

DEDICATION xi

INTRODUCTION 1

PART ONE: WHY TELEVISION ADVERTISING?

CHAPTER 1 9
TV Is Alive!

CHAPTER 2 25
Digital Delusions

CHAPTER 3 39
Bank On Big Moves

PART TWO: HOW TO BUILD WORLD-CLASS TV CAMPAIGNS

CHAPTER 4 57
Strategy: Consumers Are Changing
Faster Than Companies

CHAPTER 5 . . . . **71**

Creative: Remarkable Work
Should Work Remarkably

CHAPTER 6 . . . . **87**

People Are the Problem;
Automation Is the Answer

CHAPTER 7 . . . . **101**

Conversion: The Consumer Is In Control

CHAPTER 8 . . . . **113**

Analytics: Data Gets Twisted
Every Damn Day

CONCLUSION **127**

IS YOUR BUSINESS READY FOR TELEVISION? **131**

Dedication

THERE IS NEVER A RIGHT TIME to start a company.

The year 1996 was that time for me. I was leaving a good agency job just as we were putting an offer in for our first home, with my wife pregnant and due in three months. But there was something vital being drained from the agency I had just spent seven years loving and growing, and I needed to find that again. More on that in a minute.

After five business plans had been written and abandoned, and with confidence turning to fear, my wife, Cindy, sat down quietly next to me, now just a week before our baby was due, and asked, "How are you doing?" Her question could have been, "What the h— are you doing?" But her supportive inquiry invited my honest response: "I don't know what's next, and I'm concerned."

That short conversation uncovered the idea that led to the business I'm still running twenty-five years later. That's a long time for an entrepreneur to hang a shingle in one place. But I still love it. And she is still my hero. And that model of help has now unfolded literally thousands of times for me—the power of banding together with a team member to elevate thinking with the potential to change lives.

The mission to change lives is still the founding principle and driving purpose of our company—a bold goal from a business anchored to advertising, but one we've seen achieved again and again through the growth of our clients' companies and the advancement of the people who power those businesses.

This book resulted from the efforts of the little girl born just a week after the idea for this business was formed because of her mother. Thank you, Elena. The manuscript was brought to life by a young marketer beginning her career journey at Marketing Architects, Aiyanna. My oldest inspired her dad to venture boldly—you rock, Julia! And the "baby" of the family, Michael, asked me the questions necessary to change my life by leaving my CEO role at work (and out of our home).

This book is dedicated to the entire team at Marketing Architects who are my heroes: Paul, Brent, Rob, Angela, and the many more who are part of the transformative journey to passionately build what's next. Because it's not the marketing work we do that's kept me engaged all these years—it's the lives we've changed. I'm thankful for and proud of the talented team, great clients, valuable partners, and industry supporters who are part of this story. Thank you to all of you.

I believe advertising has the power for transformative good. You can make a strong argument that it's the most powerful form of speech. At the very least, it creates value that improves the condition of nearly every product and service on the planet.

Research from McKinsey suggests that only one in seventeen hundred companies get to the level of growth our company has achieved. (As a statistician, I must quote at least one metric before signing off on this opening.) But it's not that outcome of which I'm most proud—it's the stories of crisis and failures overcome.

So why did I leave an agency I loved to start another one? I left because the agency environment too often conspires against great teamwork and bold creative thinking by excessively pressuring the talented creators with financial, accounting, and reporting structures that suppress, rather than foster, breakthroughs. Our "All-Inclusive" model breaks that mold.

This book is dedicated to our team and to driving change into the advertising industry to support the creators who make this all possible.

—CHUCK HENGEL
CEO, Marketing Architects

Introduction

"THERE'S BEEN A CHANGE in airport operations," the voice crackled over the speaker. "Please check the monitors as you exit the plane and enter the terminal."

It had been an early flight to Kansas City. Just four years since founding a direct-response radio agency called Marketing Architects, I was traveling often and was scheduled to meet with a client that morning.

Walking into the terminal, I noticed a crowd hovering around the nearest monitor, gawking at the screen showing clouds of gray smoke billowing off the top of a skyscraper. The World Trade Center, I realized, sharing in the shock of the crowd.

"Terrorism," an older man next to me muttered, disgusted.

Terrorism? Surely not. Some sort of terrible accident, maybe. Still, it was clear air travel would be a problem for the rest of the day. I hurried to Hertz for a rental car. The man in front of me stepped up to the counter.

"How long will you need the car?" asked the salesperson.

The man reached into his suit jacket and pulled out a badge with the words *Federal Bureau of Investigation* emblazoned in gold. "I'm not sure," he said, "but I'm headed to DC."

The FBI. I couldn't believe it. What was happening? By the time I left the airport terminal, keys in hand, there were at least fifty people waiting for cars, the line stretching down the parking lot.

I attended the client meeting as scheduled. But it wasn't long before we were interrupted with instructions to turn on the news. The South Tower had collapsed, and the president had just spoken to the nation. The man at the airport had been right. The client and I sat in the conference room and watched in horror.

We ended the meeting immediately. I began the seven-hour drive home to Minneapolis, the car radio turned up. There were no songs, no shows, no commercials. Just the same terrifying news: that morning, September 11, 2001, the United States of America had been attacked.

The business implications hit me the next day. Unsure what would come next, businesses cut their advertising spend. Radio was no exception. Marketing Architects was barely beyond start-up mode at this point. There was no way we could handle all our clients leaving radio indefinitely. If we wanted to stay in business, we would have to get advertisers back on the air—and quickly.

We presented our clients with a compromise. We would guarantee performance if they maintained their spend. If they did not achieve the targeted sales goals, we would pay the difference. It was a risk but was our only way to give clients the confidence to go back on air. Seven out of eight advertisers agreed, which put us in the market for another client.

Air travel resumed, and a colleague and I booked one of the first flights to DC. If we were going to cold-call prospective clients that week, it felt important to pay our respects. We were the only passengers on the plane. Upon our arrival, Dulles airport was essentially empty. Driving into the city, we saw that not a single car traveled in the same direction as ours. DC was the last place anyone wanted to be.

The prospect we visited was angry. "You came here, with everything that's happened?" he asked.

We invited the prospect to lunch and explained that we had come to DC because we knew he needed to start advertising again to stay in business. And we believed consumers would respond if he did. By the end of the day, we once again had eight clients.

Still, we weren't hoping for much from ad performance. The company braced for a brutal stretch. But the response from consumers surprised us. The sales were three times what we expected.

We assumed our media was overclearing. After companies began pulling their advertising, it seemed like our commercials were among only a few remaining on the radio across the United States. While we typically cleared about half our media order, the loss of other advertisers likely meant our airing frequency skyrocketed. We started calling radio stations. If clients were overclearing, our agency would have to pay for it.

But the stations all said the same thing: "You're clearing the same as before. We figured you would want that capped. And honestly, we appreciate you airing anything when big-name advertisers are pulling back."

We were stunned. If clearance hadn't changed, then performance had really improved. People were responding at double the rate of just a week before. Turning to radio for news, but also eager for any semblance of normalcy and control during this time, more consumers than ever were calling the 1-800 numbers listed at the end of each commercial, ready to buy.

We had expected disaster. But it was the most successful year to date for our clients based on their advertising goals—and the fastest growth the agency had seen.

We had taken a risk in going against the status quo. But it paid off—for us, for the new employees we were able to hire, for consumers looking to regain stability and order. And for our clients.

> We had expected disaster. But it was the most successful year to date for our clients based on their advertising goals—and the fastest growth the agency had seen.

THE POWER OF ADVERTISING

It might seem strange to begin a book about TV advertising with a story from Marketing Architects' radio days, but it's important to establish something before we address TV: advertising is powerful. An integral part of our everyday lives, advertising keeps the economy churning. It transforms brands. It equips companies to better serve their customers, hire more employees, and have a greater impact on the world.

But, to borrow a cliché, with great power comes great responsibility. In advertising, we have a responsibility to society to select the types of companies we work with thoughtfully. We have a responsibility to our clients to use this incredible tool as effectively and wisely as possible. And at Marketing Architects, we have a responsibility to share the insight we've gained after more than two decades in the industry.

That's exactly why I'm writing this book. Over the years, I've learned that achieving transformative results through advertising sometimes requires moving against the crowd. Driving into DC when every other car on the road is driving out. Risking everything to keep advertisers on the air when no one else is.

Marketing Architects has never been afraid to try something new. It's why we transitioned from radio to television. We saw how radio's value for advertisers was decreasing over time, while TV's remained strong. So we scheduled a company-wide announcement, played the Buggles' "Video Killed the Radio Star" over the loudspeakers, and jumped right into figuring out how to develop a new approach to the traditional television industry.

We challenged every convention. Due to the typical high cost of launching a campaign, TV has long been viewed as a channel restricted to the biggest brands with even bigger budgets. We blew up legacy best practices to produce creative, buy media, drive consumer response, and measure results at a price point that made TV a major growth multiplier.

Today, we call our approach All-Inclusive TV. It's disrupted the high-cost structure of traditional TV agencies by providing all the services required to craft world-class campaigns while only billing for one.

THE POWER OF TV

And a lot has changed since we joined the TV space over ten years ago. Linear television viewership is decreasing, while new streaming platforms grow. Today, there's no shortage of articles declaring traditional TV dead and gone.

I see two problems with this claim. First, TV advertising is changing, not dying. It remains a powerful way to build brands and drive sales, even as it evolves into formats beyond linear.

Second, the doom and gloom around the "death

TV advertising is changing, not dying.

of linear" is premature. Many brands are so focused on the shiny new object that is streaming TV that they miss the huge opportunity remaining on traditional television.

I'm going to make a case for TV's value and share what Marketing Architects has learned from delivering this value to clients over the years. I hope this book allows you to see TV advertising in a new way and to master it. Because, when done right, television advertising can change everything for your business.

Part One

WHY TELEVISION ADVERTISING?

Chapter 1

TV IS ALIVE!

AS OFTEN AS I HAD VISITED New York City, I wasn't sure if I'd ever seen a view like this. On this day, it wasn't the classic skyline that drew my attention. Instead, I was watching the young founder of a Silicon Valley start-up called Touch of Modern sit on stage beside the CEO of multibillion-dollar exercise equipment company Peloton.

Despite leading very different companies, both leaders had invested heavily in TV advertising that year. Their brands were selected by the Video Advertising Bureau (VAB) to be featured in their "You Innovate, TV Elevates" founders campaign, which profiles the success stories of the innovative leaders behind profitable direct-to-consumer companies.

As an insights-driven research and marketing company, and the voice of the video industry, VAB wanted to create a national multiscreen commercial promoting TV itself in order to encourage more marketers to test the channel. And the company wanted that commercial to highlight TV campaigns from Touch of Modern and Peloton as examples of the medium's power. The stories of these two companies would showcase the important role TV advertising played in driving brand awareness, consumer action, and business growth for their digitally native, data-driven businesses.

In my opinion, only a marketing channel like TV could accomplish this feat. Only TV could bring these leaders and innovators together from vastly different businesses and opposite sides of the country to celebrate their success advertising on the same channel.

That said, nearly every third article on advertising these days reads something like "TV's days are numbered." Occasionally, an article is more blatant, declaring TV's death in its headline. But rumors of TV's irrelevance have circulated for years. Declining viewership due to cord-cutting, changing consumer habits, and the rise of new entertainment platforms has contributed to this narrative.

The truth? TV is not just alive. It's thriving.

TV advertising has evolved exponentially since the industry's start in 1941, when the Bulova Watch Company aired the first television commercial. It was black and white, ten seconds long, and it aired only in New York. It's hard to imagine such a commercial today, when the biggest brands dedicate billions of dollars to creative production every year.

I've watched drastic transformations take place across the entire advertising industry since founding a direct-response radio agency over two decades ago. The pace of change in just the last five years—or even the past six months—is staggering.

Companies and platforms have come and gone. Targeting and measurement capabilities have completely transformed. We experience media in an entirely new way and have shifted expectations for advertising. All this change isn't showing any sign of slowing.

In 1997, I was stuck in choosing among a few names for the business I wanted to build, so I resolved to draw the name out of a hat. The result? Marketing Architects. I stuck with it because both words communicated a pairing of art and science that is critical to our success. The best marketers and the best architects are both creative and technical, inventive and precise.

Over the last two and a half decades, our name hasn't changed, but our agency has. When the glory days of radio faded, while TV surged, we followed the trend and refocused only on TV. As years passed, employees, clients, and business plans came and went—and then came back again as we entered new eras. We built our own custom, state-of-the-art technology after throwing our hands up in frustration at what was available on the market. Most recently, we transitioned from a centralized Minneapolis office to a still-tight-knit but now remote team working across the country. Even so, one thing hasn't changed much at all—TV's power to transform brands and drive extraordinary business growth.

After seeing firsthand what TV has accomplished for our clients, I have full confidence in its impact. Whether the aim is to shift a business model, achieve aggressive sales goals, or increase stock price, TV has proven to be effective. In fact, in all my years in the marketing industry, I have not found another channel that delivers results quite like TV.

Consider TV's scale and reach. It has unparalleled ability to simultaneously connect with a small-business owner in Santa Fe, a teacher in Boston, and a corporate executive in Seattle. Worldwide, TV reaches more people

> In all my years in the marketing industry, I have not found another channel that delivers results quite like TV.

than any other content-based channel.[1] No other single marketing medium has that same power. Take it from the more than 120 million American households with televisions—*120 million.* That's nearly 94 percent of all homes in the United States, and most of those homes have more than one TV. TV is everywhere. That much is undeniable. Television, and its advertising, shapes the way we as consumers learn new information, stay connected to the world around us, and perceive our own society.

I'm a big fan of television advertising, but I promise you this book isn't merely a love letter to TV. It's a reflection on television's triumphs—and challenges. And it's a humble guide to using TV as effectively as possible.

A TOUCH OF TV

Founded in 2012, the San Francisco–based e-commerce app Touch of Modern caters to male trendsetters with curated collections of unique, cutting-edge products. Beyond that, they don't follow many category rules. You are equally likely to discover a one-of-a-kind high-scale watch, a mobile infrared camera system, and a portable tree house while browsing their site.

Inc. 5000 named the brand one of the five hundred fastest-growing private companies in America two years in a row. By the end of 2015, Touch of Modern had increased its annual orders thirtyfold and transformed from a four-person start-up to a company of one hundred employees casually receiving its one millionth order. Today, the platform boasts over twenty-two million users.

---

1   Karin von Abrams, "The Global Media Intelligence Report 2020," Inside Intelligence, October 15, 2020, https://www.emarketer.com/content/global-media-intelligence-2020.

All this is to say that Touch of Modern knows a thing or two about achieving stunning growth. They lead the pack by pushing the limits of what's possible.

For them, TV advertising was an experiment. Could an app targeting a younger demographic of stylish millennials drive results through TV? In true entrepreneurial spirit, they were willing to find out.

When Touch of Modern first launched TV in 2017, they had high expectations and aggressive growth goals. At first, campaign results were lackluster. The campaign showed early promise, but it wasn't meeting Touch of Modern's aggressive goals. For TV to remain a core marketing channel, they needed to do better.

Surprising to some, young disruptors can do especially well on TV. In 2018, "emerging" brands saw a 93 percent average lift in website traffic after launching television.[2] And Touch of Modern sat comfortably within a direct-to-consumer category that's popular on TV. Theoretically, television was exactly what they needed to gain familiarity with a broader audience, including purchase influencers and undiscovered customer segments. We believed the marketing channel wasn't the problem. There was real potential with the right approach.

Touch of Modern asked us to take a second swing at their TV campaign. We approached this opportunity as about more than producing beautiful creative or clearing prime time airings. It was about building a lasting brand through TV. We saw an opportunity to prove TV still stands as a relevant marketing channel for a young, trendsetting business. How would we know if the campaign worked? Touch of Modern's ultimate focus was driving revenue through new

2   "Direct Outcomes," VAB, accessed March 4, 2021, https://thevab.com/insight/DirectOutcomes.

customer growth. With a move as big as TV, they wanted dramatic results. If TV couldn't keep up with the brand's goals, it wasn't worth their investment.

We began work to redesign and scale the campaign. With new, pretested creative and a media plan built and approved by artificial intelligence, we relaunched Touch of Modern's TV.

Touch of Modern's top concern was that the channel lacked the accountability of digital advertising—an area in which they were more comfortable. They quickly discovered TV can be accurately tracked and measured with the right technology. If a campaign is set up correctly, the advertiser should absolutely know how it is impacting their brand and bottom line.

After the relaunch of TV, Touch of Modern quickly saw their metrics improve. Their Google search costs decreased. Cost per customer dropped. Average order value increased. Sales began to lift and then take off. Investors expressed interest, awards were won, major-label merchandisers wanted their products on the platform, and press inquiries poured in. TV catapulted Touch of Modern to a level of fame the brand had never expected.

> If a campaign is set up correctly, the advertiser should absolutely know how it is impacting their brand and bottom line.

That's when the VAB reached out. They were launching their annual founders campaign, and "You Innovate, TV Elevates" wanted to feature Touch of Modern as a successful and savvy direct-to-consumer brand in growth mode. Working closely with Touch of Modern's leadership team, the VAB developed a multiscreen commercial explaining the brand's story—and how TV went from an experiment to their primary marketing channel. The commercial aired on sixty TV networks and almost all local TV markets through the fall of 2019.

"TV is now the biggest portion of our marketing spend," said Jerry Hum, Touch of Modern cofounder and executive chairman, in an interview. "If I were advising another company, I would tell them to test TV. But as a competitor, I would tell them not to."[3]

The very fact that a digital-native brand targeting millennials could see incredible returns on TV advertising is evidence of TV's continued relevance. That a start-up brand from San Francisco would be featured in a national campaign alongside one of the most well-known brands today is proof of TV's power.

The real beauty of the VAB campaign was that it exposed major TV misconceptions to the advertising industry as exactly that—misconceptions.

BATTLING MISCONCEPTIONS

Perhaps the greatest challenge facing traditional TV today is the issue of viewership. Is anyone watching? Are vast and varied audiences still browsing channels? Are the glory days of linear TV long past? As streaming services take center stage and cord cutters become a far less exclusive club, advertisers understandably question the lasting power and relevance of linear TV—including local and national cable, broadcast, syndication, and satellite television.

Those questions can be answered with simple statistics. The average American consumes nearly six hours of video content in a

---

3   "Touch of Modern TV Campaign Helps Direct-to-Consumer Company Reach Major Milestone," Marketing Architects, July 9, 2019, https://www.marketingarchitects.com/blog/touch-of-modern-tv-campaign.

day.[4] Six hours! That's a quarter of the day. In six hours, I can fly from San Francisco to Atlanta and still have time to catch a movie once I arrive. That's how much screen time fills our lives.

Here's more: audiences ages twelve to seventeen spend most of their screen time watching content on a smartphone or internet-connected device. However, TV viewers ages eighteen to thirty-four spend nearly two hours watching on a traditional television set, and those ages thirty-five and older watch over five hours daily. So, yes, if your primary purchase audience is the average American teenager, linear TV might not be the ideal fit for your brand. But if not, your customers are watching more content than ever—and much of it still on linear TV.

What about all the supposed cord cutters opting for streaming services rather than paying for cable? For simplicity's sake, I'll wrap under the term "streaming TV" all of the following: advanced TV, over-the-top television, set-top-box video on demand, and address-able. This category has its own opportunities, especially as technology continues to improve. We've established that people watch more content than ever. The only change is how some are accessing that content. And advertising remains an option on many video-on-demand platforms like Hulu or Amazon Prime Video.

It's a misconception that streaming is a TV killer. Streaming is simply a new branch of TV. Streaming TV's benefits include watchability across essentially any internet-connected device, which means that your ad could be viewed not just on a television, but also on a smartphone, laptop, or tablet. Audience targeting is also possible at a level that's difficult to achieve with linear.

However, the very newness of streaming—the quality that makes

---

4   "The State of Traditional TV: Updates with Q1 2020 Data," Marketing Charts, September 14, 2020, https://www.marketingcharts.com/featured-105414.

it such an attractive, shiny option for marketers—also represents its downside. Publishers struggle with ad frequency management and capping—wasting both impressions and valuable ad dollars.[5] Measurement hasn't fully been fleshed out either. When you target by individual households, for example, evaluating response quickly becomes complicated. Admittedly, recent steps forward on the measurement front suggest this is a solvable problem given the appropriate time and technology. But we're not there just yet.

And for many brands, the precise targeting capabilities streaming offers don't meet cost-cutting expectations. If, in a group of one hundred people, you only share your message with one person, you'd better have high confidence in the one with whom you've chosen to connect. Quite frankly, that's more easily said than done. Predicting consumer buying preferences before they know themselves always has some element of chance.

That brings us back to the beauty of linear television's mass reach. When you can connect with all one hundred people for the same price as targeting just one, why not advertise to all one hundred? Why not tip the odds of converting a new customer in your favor?

Add to these considerations the fact that instead of choosing streaming as an uncomplicated, inexpensive alternative to dozens of unused cable channels, many households are simply adding streaming services to their preexisting cable subscriptions. Prices continue rising for major players like Netflix and Hulu even as new competitors enter the picture. Given the launch of Disney+, HBO Max, and NBC's Peacock, the streaming competitive landscape is far from the simple world it once was.

---

5   Andrew Blustein, "These are the problems holding CTV advertising back" The Drum, February 26, 2019, https://www.thedrum.com/news/2019/02/26/these-are-the-problems-holding-ctv-advertising-back.

This complexity is reflected in how people watch—or don't watch—content. Over 70 percent of households that subscribe to any streaming service subscribe to more than one.[6] Almost 20 percent subscribe to four or more. The bills can amount to more than cable did in the first place. Plus, as new streaming services launch, subscription fatigue increases.[7]

It's the paradox of choice. Too many options can lead to decision paralysis. Imagine strolling through your local supermarket without a shopping list in hand. Browsing for what you really want, what will make you the happiest and cost you the least, suddenly becomes an overwhelming chore. In the same way, viewers not only have to choose what to watch but also on which platform to watch. Over 20 percent of streaming-service users give up on watching anything if they're not able to make up their minds. For advertisers, that's bad news. Not watching content also means viewers are not seeing your commercial.[8]

And even as streaming platforms continue battling for dominance while consumers search wearily, remotes in hands, cable companies are not letting customers defect without a fight. Offering more flexible package options with increased selectivity, personalization, and pricing has become one popular retention strategy.

The situation is anything but simple.

Consumers are discovering that for themselves. A surprising

---

6   James K. Willcox, "The Cord-Cutting Decision Is Tougher These Days. Here's What You Need to Know," Consumer Reports, July 29, 2019, https://www.consumerreports.org/tv-service/cord-cutting-decision-what-you-need-to-know/.

7   Todd Spangler, "'Subscription Fatigue': Nearly Half of US Consumers Frustrated by Streaming Explosion, Study Finds," Variety, March 18, 2019, https://variety.com/2019/digital/news/streaming-subscription-fatigue-us-consumers-deloitte-study-1203166046/.

8   Dade Hayes, "Streaming Overload? Nielsen Report Finds Average Viewer Takes 7 Minutes to Pick What to Watch; Just One-Third Bother to Check Menu," Deadline, July 1, 2019, https://deadline.com/2019/07/streaming-overload-netflix-nielsen-report-average-viewer-takes-7-minutes-to-pick-what-to-watch-1202640213/.

number are still flipping through channels—streaming services or not. Streaming consistently captures only a minority. In 2019, even millennials watched more linear television than streamed content.[9]

Based on the same investment, a brand will reach ten times more people through linear than through over-the-top. Some may worry that broad reach wastes impressions on uninterested consumers, but that's not the case if you buy quality media targeted by region and demographics. You control the networks and programs on which your commercial airs. Linear TV is still a mass-reach medium, but there is a capability for selectivity and strategy when it comes to reaching certain customers with your brand messaging. And ad relevance remains higher on linear TV than on streaming TV. Nearly half of US internet users report linear TV as being where they are most likely to see a relevant ad. Only 12 percent listed streaming TV.[10]

Linear television still holds significant value. It likely will for some time. Advertisers and agencies know this. Streaming TV options like over-the-top continue to generate just a fraction of linear's annual ad revenue.[11]

Linear TV's reputation as the most effective brand-building channel stands untarnished to this day. A 2018 study found that 70 percent of businesses considered TV their key brand-building medium.[12] And the biggest, most famous brands today have used and

---

9   Julia Stoll, "Number of TV households in the United States from seasons 2000-2001 to seasons 2019-2020," statista, January 13, 2021, https://www.statista.com/statistics/243789/number-of-tv-households-in-the-us/.

10   Blake Droesch, "TV Ads Still More Relevant to Consumers Than Streaming Video Ads," eMarketer, May 15, 2019, https://www.emarketer.com/content/tv-ads-still-more-relevant-to-consumers-than-streaming-video-ads.

11   Chelsea Layzell, "OTT Advertising UX Takeaways and Lessons from Hulu and Roku," Zemoga, Inc., February 4, 2020, https://www.zemoga.com/insights/blog/ott-advertising/.

12   "TV still central to building brands," WARC, July 3, 2018, https://www.warc.com/newsandopinion/news/tv_still_central_to_building_brands/40139.

continue to use television to connect with customers and expand their brand value. Think Apple. Coca-Cola. Nike. Procter & Gamble. All spend millions on television each year. The list goes on to include Amazon Prime, Disney+, HBO, Hulu, and Sling. Yes, even streaming platforms know the power of linear TV, collectively spending over a quarter of a billion dollars on the medium in a single year.[13] Surely these powerhouse brands must be getting something right.

TV provides advertising opportunities to create a full brand experience for which a print or digital ad simply isn't equipped. What other marketing medium combines so many sensory elements—audio, imagery, and motion—and then distributes them at scale? A well-crafted commercial can weave all the available elements into a complete and compelling story, one that captivates, engages, and ideally calls the viewer to act.

> Even streaming platforms know the power of linear TV, collectively spending over a quarter of a billion dollars on the medium in a single year. Surely these powerhouse brands must be getting something right.

With linear TV, viewers are more willing to go along for the ride. TV is considered a far more trustworthy source of information than either digital video or social media.[14] As a traditional

---

13   "Confessions of a Fortune Teller," Ad Contrarian Newsletter, accessed March 4, 2021, http://createsend.com/t/d-BA1720CF3E8A53862540EF23F30FEDED.

14   Chris Myers, "New Group Research Examines Consumer Trust in Digital Marketing," GroupM, March 30, 2020, https://www.groupm.com/new-groupm-research-examines-consumer-trust-digital-marketing/.

form of advertising, TV's long-standing reputation as the chosen medium of major brands serves as an advantage. Additionally, the perceived high costs and numerous quality and accuracy checkpoints at the company, agency, and network levels mean consumers are more trusting of what they learn on TV and more likely to associate the brands they see there with positive feelings. Merely being on linear TV connotes credibility and prestige.

Next, consider that most people make decisions—including purchase decisions—emotionally.[15] Fifty-eight percent of consumers report that TV advertising is the marketing channel most likely to make them feel emotional. Less than 10 percent of consumers say the same of social media advertising, including digital video on social media.[16] As a result, most advertisers prefer TV, even over digital video, when it comes to protecting and promoting brand reputation.[17]

As streaming's audiences grow and technology improves, many of these principles of linear television will also apply. Already, we've found streaming can be an ideal complement to a scaled national campaign in order to extend reach, increase campaign effectiveness, and target specific customer groups. But while streaming is a new and exciting superpower, many advertisers know that linear TV is ultimately the hero of the story.

---

15   Logan Chierotti, "Harvard Professor Says 95% of Purchasing Decisions Are Subconscious," Inc., March 26, 2018, https://www.inc.com/logan-chierotti/harvard-professor-says-95-of-purchasing-decisions-are-subconscious.html.

16   "Be Still My Viewing Heart," VAB, accessed March 4, 2021, https://thevab.com/insight/be-still-my-viewing-heart.

17   Nick Troiano, "Iconic Brand Advertising on TV Isn't Going Anywhere," Ad Age, June 14, 2018, https://adage.com/article/cadent/iconic-brand-advertising-tv/313717.

TELEVISION TODAY

The reliability and trust TV advertising creates for a brand is more important than ever during times of crisis. The reassurance and emotional connection established through television improves public opinion, positively impacts brand image, and can help a brand navigate through frightening times—for both businesses and consumers. Touch of Modern learned just that when the COVID-19 pandemic shocked the world in spring of 2020.

Leading up to 2020, Touch of Modern had continued seeing strong return on their TV campaigns. But as the pandemic disrupted the advertising industry—and just about everything else—TV had another opportunity to have an even bigger impact on Touch of Modern's business.

We knew Touch of Modern's ad messaging had to make a sudden shift. And that shift needed to happen in weeks, not months. The turnaround had to be quick to capitalize on a unique media opportunity. As many large-name brand advertisers began to pull back on spend, more inventory was available for less. This would save the brand valuable ad dollars during a time when uncertainty was at an all-time high.

Touch of Modern curated a store within their site to highlight products intended to make quarantining at home a little less restrictive. The collection included exercise equipment, work essentials, and home entertainment products. We then planned and launched a new spot highlighting the "Shelter at Home" store.

The response was instantaneous.

The campaign contributed to a 35 percent year-over-year increase in total revenue from May to June. Touch of Modern began seeing conversion rates typically only experienced during the peak holiday season. Many sales belonged to new customers. Even in the middle of a worldwide crisis, linear TV pushed the brand forward. And it continues to do so today.

Touch of Modern is just one brand of many that has harnessed the power of TV to attain both short- and long-term success.

TV is still changing. That much can't be denied. But in many ways, that's a good thing. TV's opportunities are expanding. More brands are testing the channel, and people are watching ads in a variety of new ways. So, while the headlines persist in proclaiming TV's demise, the results brands see from TV, both linear and streaming, prove otherwise. Linear television remains a powerful tool, and streaming points to a world of new TV possibilities down the road. The very fact that TV's been able to adapt is exactly why it's still relevant—and will be for many years to come.

Unfortunately, digital advertising seems to disagree. In fact, it wouldn't mind setting TV aside for good. But trading traditional marketing channels for digital is more dangerous than many know.

Chapter 2

DIGITAL DELUSIONS

I THANKED THE EXECUTIVE LEADERS of CBS Radio for their time. I had just finished an hour-long presentation explaining why the CBS network should continue working with Marketing Architects—instead of Google—to sell their radio inventory.

A decade into Marketing Architects' existence as a radio agency, Google had become our fiercest competitor. Google wanted to expand beyond their successful search advertising business into offline channels. Radio was the tech giant's first foray in this expansion, and they were clearly committed to making it work. In January 2006, they made a big move. Google bought dMarc, a firm whose focus on automation echoed our own media-buying approach.

And the battle began.

For years, Marketing Architects had worked to build mutually beneficial relationships with radio networks. It's how we delivered superior rates for our clients. To undermine our approach, Google repeatedly tried to block us from networks by making exclusive deals. Not many networks agreed. Google struggled to get traction as the radio networks recognized that our partnership offered them more value. However, we knew if we lost CBS Radio, we would be in trouble.

At the time, CBS provided over 20 percent of our entire radio media inventory. From salespeople to management, we worked with more than nine hundred employees inside the CBS Radio corporation. We felt confident in the strength of our relationships. Even so, the allure of working with a big name like Google had us worried about the network's decision.

Leaving the CBS conference room, I heard a voice from down the hall. "Chuck. Hey, Chuck."

The CEO of CBS Radio had followed me out. "I know this is an important meeting for you," he said, "and I can't formally share our decision. But I can tell you it was a great presentation, and we really value the relationship we have with your company." He paused and then smiled. "And there's no way in hell Google's getting our inventory."

CBS chose to continue our relationship, and Google lost one battle. But the war for control of the radio space raged on.

A year later, the National Association of Broadcasters (NAB) hosted their annual trade show in Las Vegas. All major TV and radio stations attended. The event gathered the best companies in broadcast advertising and featured the latest industry technology. Google claimed a massive booth at one side of the room.

I attended the trade show to recruit radio stations, but curiosity drew me to Google's booth. Two Google employees blocked my way. "You're not welcome here," they said.

Being escorted away from Google's booth seemed extreme at the time, but they had reason to be defensive—because we outlasted Google in radio. They didn't emphasize attribution the way we did. Their creative focused more on beautiful soundtracks than driving sales. And they never could quite replicate our relationship-based media-buying approach—the one we would later modify to buy TV inventory.

Google's failure to reach radio glory reminded me of that presentation for CBS. Somehow, even when it seemed Google had everything in its favor, that CEO had known. He'd known that for all the unlimited cash, data, and technology Google claimed, their approach was one sided. And eventually, everyone who bought into Google's radio ambitions simply because ... well, it was Google ... would discover their error.

Google is great at what Google does best: search engine advertising. When they expanded into a new realm requiring different creative, technology, and relationship building, they failed. They tried to do too much with a single strategy.

Today, marketers often fall into a similar trap by trying to make online advertising accomplish all their marketing goals. They put their brands at risk by placing all their bets with companies like Google and Facebook. A belief in digital's ability to "do it all" has led more than one business to the start-up cemetery.

DIGITAL'S UPSIDES

Saying we live in a digital world is an understatement. We work, learn, pay bills, publish and consume content, communicate, and shop online. A more accurate phrase? We *live digitally*. Naturally, this affects advertising. I'll say it repeatedly throughout this book: advertising must follow the consumer. And today's consumers are online.

The first banner ad appeared in 1994 on a site owned by *Wired*. AT&T paid for the ad, which lived on the site for three months. It transported those who clicked on the image to a landing page featuring rainbow-colored stripes and a bold blue link promoting the opportunity to learn more about AT&T. With a click-through rate of 44 percent—an impossible number by today's standards—the ad was deemed an instant success.[18]

Everyone wanted in. Digital began evolving at rates the advertising industry had never seen. Pop-up ads. Pay-per-click. Paid search. Social media advertising. Improved measurement, more consumers spending time online, and increasing online ad availability helped digital surpass other channels at a record pace. In 2020, half of all advertising expenditure went to the internet, overtaking TV's spot as the top advertising medium.[19]

There's good reason to include digital in your marketing mix. For starters, digital is extremely measurable. Tracking impressions and conversions is easy online, so advertisers can keep an eye on their campaign's performance and ROI. For businesses looking to account for every dollar they spend on advertising, digital is a marketer's dream come true. And if performance isn't where it should be, it's fairly simple to shift your strategy accordingly. Marketers can run hundreds of thousands of advertising tests through digital. Different headlines, hero images, and colors can be tested and tweaked instantly. And it's easy to review the results of each change. This flexibility makes digital less intimidating to try in the first place.

Advertisers also appreciate digital's ability to share quality content for less—building communities of fans and followers with similar interests at a budget-friendly cost. With greater accessibility than traditional media, digital platforms even the playing field for modestly sized companies to compete with big-brand advertising.

18   Karla Cook, "A Brief History of Online Advertising," Hubspot, September 12, 2016, https://blog.hubspot.com/marketing/history-of-online-advertising.

19   A. Guttmann, "Distribution of advertising spending worldwide in 2020, by medium," statista, January 12, 2021, https://www.statista.com/statistics/376260/global-ad-spend-distribution-by-medium/.

But perhaps the most acclaimed aspect of digital is its targeting capabilities. The idea that you can reach those already primed to be your next customers is incredible. You choose your audience's age, gender, income and occupation, and interests based on past search history. Is your target audience a thirtysomething male professional who loves the outdoors, travel, and barbecue? Digital advertising finds and reaches only those fitting the profile. What marketers wouldn't want to spend valuable impressions on only those who are most likely to make it worth their time and money?

DIGITAL'S DOWNSIDES

Theoretically, digital advertising seems like a dream come true. But in practice, targeting at such an extreme level isn't the solution everyone wishes it were. The problem? To target consumers so precisely, the data deciding who, where, and how you target must be impeccable. And unfortunately, that's rarely the case.

Research increasingly proves tight targeting does not drive ideal results. It ignores large groups of current and future customers thanks to faulty assumptions about who is best suited to buy a brand's product or service. Plus, the more targeted a campaign, the more expensive it is. You pay more to reach fewer people.

Besides, just because marketers love digital's targeting capabilities doesn't mean consumers do. In fact, many are uncomfortable, concerned the internet knows them a little too well. Recent California legislation proves this discomfort is growing. The California Consumer Privacy Act (CCPA) of 2018 requires businesses to clearly explain their privacy practices and provide consumers the opportunity to both delete personal information that's been collected and opt out of the sale of that information.[20] And in 2020, the California Privacy Rights Act, known as Prop 24, was passed, demanding that consumers be allowed to opt out of targeted advertising based on online behaviors beginning in 2023.[21] It also established the California Privacy Protection Agency to enforce the statute. Without all that data, digital's primary advantage is impaired.

> Just because marketers love digital's targeting capabilities doesn't mean consumers do. In fact, many are uncomfortable, concerned the internet knows them a little too well.

Even though these specific laws only apply to California residents, the rest of the country is still seriously impacted since nearly all major US tech companies operate out of California. As a result, many businesses choose to extend those rules across the nation. Plus, more than one state has discussed following California's lead. Even so, the United States is trailing behind when it comes to consumer privacy laws—there's much stronger legislation already in effect in Europe. Consumer privacy is highly prioritized there, and businesses already feel the sting of limited targeting capabilities.

There are not just privacy concerns causing problems for digital advertisers. Due to its low barrier of entry for businesses of all sizes,

---

20   "California Consumer Privacy Act (CCPA)," State of California Department of Justice Office of the Attorney General, accessed March 4, 2021, https://oag.ca.gov/privacy/ccpa.

21   Kate Kaye, "California data privacy law, Prop 24, set to have major impact on ad targeting," The Drum, October 30, 2020, https://www.thedrum.com/news/2020/10/30/california-data-privacy-law-prop-24-set-have-major-impact-ad-targeting?utm_source=morning_brew.

the internet is flooded with digital advertising. There's too much information for consumers to sift through for much to feel relevant or noteworthy. This is especially true for younger audiences—despite claims that digital is the ideal way to reach them. In fact, one study found consumers aged twenty to forty experience little to no effect from viewing online display ads.[22] Digital ads are so numerous that many of us have trained our brains to tune them out. On top of that, the creative restrictions of a pop-up or display ad leaves little room to develop strong memorability. Two decades after the first banner ad, the average click-through rate dropped to just 0.14 percent in North America.[23]

The flood of content means digital is not only less impactful—it's also increasingly more expensive. The competition for ad space is overwhelming. And as the costs of paid search skyrocket while more advertisers fight for the same keywords, Google simultaneously raises ad prices. Major tech companies meet their revenue goals by upping cost-per-click rates. Nearly 80 percent of Google's annual revenue comes from advertising. They certainly aren't above demanding every dollar they can get from digital-dependent advertisers.

Consider the "Google Tax," a fee initially imposed on tech giants by European Union lawmakers in April of 2020 to check the companies' growing market control. The advertisers are the ones who ended up paying. In response to the tax, Google raised digital ad fees by 2 percent in the UK and 5 percent in Austria and Turkey.[24] Brands

22   Tim Hwang, *Subprime Attention Crisis: Advertising and the Time Bomb at the Heart of the Internet* (Farrar, Straus and Giroux: 2020).

23   Jack Loechner, "North America Banner Click Through Rate Up To 0.14%," Research Brief, December 6, 2016, https://www.mediapost.com/publications/article/290285/north-america-banner-click-through-rate-up-to-014.html.

24   Mark Sweney, "Google's advertiser will take the hit from UK digital service tax," The Guardian, September 1, 2020, https://www.theguardian.com/media/2020/sep/01/googles-advertisers-will-take-the-hit-from-uk-digital-service-tax.

that rely completely on digital for advertising have no leverage with which to push back on these price increases.

For these advertisers, brand safety is also a major concern. It's not just that your ad might appear beside inappropriate user content. Simply being on a platform associates your brand with the latest news—good or bad—about that platform. And when that's your only marketing channel, that's the only association consumers have for your brand.

Facebook especially has been criticized again and again for its management of hateful material. The summer of 2020 found consumers more frustrated than ever in this regard. Emotions peaked as the coronavirus pandemic and correlating economic downturn brought new fear and uncertainty into the world. And when that spring's civil unrest and contentious political campaign hit social media—and not in a good way—consumers called for companies to act.

Brands ranging from The North Face to Unilever to Ben & Jerry's enacted advertising boycotts on Facebook, Instagram, Twitter, and even YouTube. At the same time, news outlets blasted headlines showcasing a Capitol Hill interrogation of Google, Facebook, and Amazon. When the tech giants argued they were not part of a monopoly, consumers simply rolled their eyes. Trust in the platforms sank to new lows.[25] By association, brands that continued to advertise on Facebook or Instagram also faced scrutiny. Having to defend your use of an advertising channel to the very consumers you're trying to convert into customers isn't what any marketer wants for their brand.

In late June of 2020, Facebook committed to a brand safety audit and announced increased restrictions on political and hateful

25   Ina Fried, "Exclusive: Global trust in the tech industry is slipping," Axios, February 25, 2020, https://www.axios.com/big-tech-industry-global-trust-9b7c6c3c-98f1-4e80-8275-cf52446b1515.html.

content, banning hundreds of extremist groups.[26] But it was only because big-name advertisers boasted a diverse marketing portfolio that they were able to boycott the platform in the first place. Many small- to medium-sized companies were unable to pull their digital ad spend because their reliance on the channel for generating revenue was too great. More small advertisers joined the platform and increased spending, resulting in Facebook's total profits growing, not decreasing, during the boycott.

Digital's struggle to protect brand reputations is nothing new. Think of Google's 2017 YouTube controversy after the platform faced outrage from advertisers who discovered their ads played beside controversial and extremist content. Since then, YouTube has instituted numerous restrictions to monitor content shared on their platform. But the very nature of a platform that promotes user-generated materials means it's not always possible to catch everything. For especially cautious brands, YouTube allows marketers to choose the subjects beside which their advertising plays, but that comes with an increased cost. This gives brands greater, though not complete, control. However, restricting the types of content on which your ad is shown limits your reach on an already reach-challenged channel. You pay more for fewer impressions.

And how many of those impressions are true leads in the first place? How many become actual customers? Online ad fraud is a bigger issue than many want to admit. In fact, an Adobe study found 28 percent of digital advertising's impact is fake.[27] As of October

26   Rachel Winicov, "After Monthlong Boycott, Which Brands Are Coming Back to Facebook?" Adweek, July 31, 2020, https://www.adweek.com/brand-marketing/facebook-boycott-which-brands-coming-back/.

27   Tim Hwang, *Subprime Attention Crisis: Advertising and the Time Bomb at the Heart of the Internet* (FSG Originals x Logic, Farrar, Straus and Giroux,2020).

2020, 15 percent of digital ad costs still go to unknown sources.[28] Bots impersonate users by visiting sites where they "view" advertisements, creating an "impression" the advertiser will have to pay for without gaining any value. Bots can even mislead brands into believing they're interacting with real people by clicking and scrolling on a page. In 2020, Facebook faced a lawsuit complaining that the platform had charged for "clicks" from fake accounts.[29]

Interested customers can also be faked when bots use real information gathered in data breaches to fill out online lead forms. Add to this frightening scenario fake social media accounts and fake followers. Even sales can be faked by tricking an attribution platform that measures online sales.[30]

Digital is overrun with faulty data, making its real impact a lot more difficult to confidently determine.

Digital is overrun with faulty data, making its real impact a lot more difficult to confidently determine.

---

28   Joe Mandese, "ANA: 15% of Digital Ad Costs Going to 'Unknown'," MediaPost, October 21, 2020, https://www.mediapost.com/publications/article/357052/ana-15-of-digital-ad-costs-going-to-unknown.html.

29   Wendy Davis, "Facebook Must Face Lawsuit over Ad Clicks from Fake Accounts," MediaPost, November 12, 2020, https://www.mediapost.com/publications/article/357759/facebook-must-face-lawsuit-over-ad-clicks-from-fak.html.

30   Augustine Fou, "How Much of Digital Is Fakery? Probably More Than Marketers Think," Forbes, June 23, 2020, www.forbes.com/sites/augustine-fou/2020/06/23/how-much-of-digital-is-fakery-probably-more-than-marketers-think/?sh=5efc87934cf7.

THE REAL RISK OF DIGITAL ADVERTISING

The real problem isn't digital itself. Online advertising is a relevant and useful tool. It's an excellent bottom-of-the-funnel marketing channel. If used correctly, it can attract new customers at an appropriate cost. The danger arises when a brand closes its eyes to digital's shortcomings and becomes overly reliant on this single medium.

Just as you wouldn't build a house with only a hammer, you can't create a complete marketing strategy with a single—and very fallible—channel. It's always safer to diversify the marketing mediums your brand depends on for growth. It is possible to reap digital's benefits and alleviate its pitfalls by pairing it with a very different channel: TV.

Like magnets and relationships, opposites also attract in advertising. Sharing content on both Facebook and Twitter does not constitute an omnichannel approach. For the best results, implement both traditional and digital media. The channels complement each other; their differences make them stronger together. Working in tandem, the two can drive short- and long-term results for greater return on your ad investment. It's why Marketing Architects clients who have relied heavily on digital experience dramatic success upon diversifying their marketing mix with TV. Television and digital can work together for improved effectiveness, a higher campaign ROI, and a more well-rounded marketing strategy.

TV AND DIGITAL ARE BETTER TOGETHER

How does pairing TV and digital work in practice? Let's say you own a company that provides everyday items for small businesses. You dedicate hundreds of thousands of dollars to paid search each month in order to compete for general keywords like "office supplies."

You'd like to grow your brand, but fighting for control over search terms is a never-ending battle. Your marketing budget is nearly spent. Reach is limited. Growth becomes increasingly difficult.

Here's where TV makes all the difference.

Even with a serious digital investment, only those who physically type "office supplies" into their search bar will discover your ad. What about a consumer like one we'll call Taylor, who works from home? She doesn't think she needs the typical materials many small businesses require. She isn't going to search for "office supplies." Instead, she might search for individual products as she needs them.

Suppose that you split your marketing budget between digital and TV advertising. You have a commercial airing on national television, reaching a mass audience. Between back-to-back episodes of *Law & Order*, Taylor sees this commercial. She immediately associates your brand with legitimacy. Just because you're on TV, she considers your brand to be trustworthy enough to investigate more. And she realizes something else: there are ways she could improve her home office.

Ninety-four percent of people watch TV with a smartphone in hand, making it a more popular TV-watching accessory than even the remote.[31] Taylor pulls out her phone. And like the nearly 70 percent of second-screen users who use their phone to search for what they see on TV, she navigates to the website listed at the end of your ad.[32] She browses the site until she spots it: the perfect ergonomic desk chair she's been missing. Immediately, Taylor orders the chair and plans to pick it up the next day. You have a new customer—thanks to TV.

And Taylor isn't the only new customer you see after your com-

31   "Mobile and TV: Between the Screens," Facebook for Business, July 10, 2017, https://www.facebook.com/business/news/insights/mobile-and-tv-between-the-screens.

32   "Most popular smartphone activities of second screen users in the United States while watching TV as of January 2019," statista, February 4, 2021, https://www.statista.com/statistics/455377/smartphone-usage-while-watching-tv/.

mercial airs. In the short term, website traffic increases immediately after an airing. And traffic driven by TV boasts especially high engagement rates. Visitors return an average of 2.3 more times, significantly increasing website lift week over week.

Long-term results of TV's impact on web traffic are equally exciting. We've seen anywhere from 1.5 to 4 times more traffic after a single airing. Plus, Marketing Architects clients regularly find that customers from TV provide greater long-term value than those who've arrived at their site by clicking on a display ad. TV-attributable customers experience more of your brand for longer while watching the commercial. They evaluate your message and intentionally choose to take action by looking online. And you don't have to worry about fake impressions or bots when your customers come from television.

But what about your paid search? What value does that have if customers are bypassing your search terms to go straight to your website? Here's another scenario: suppose Taylor sees the TV commercial but doesn't type the exact URL into her phone. Instead, she simply searches the name of your company. Since you planned for this, you have paid search ads associated with your own brand name. So when Taylor searches for your company, an ad pops up right away. She clicks. Browses your site. Discovers that amazing desk chair.

The paid search ads for your brand are significantly less expensive because the keywords for a specific company name face far less competition than an entire category. This new approach both reduces costs and drastically improves your share of search—a metric that tells you how much online search traffic within a specific category goes to your business.[33] With a higher share of search, you can expect brand growth.

33   James Swift, "Share of search: the new most important brand metric?" Contagious, August 6, 2020, https://www.contagious.com/news-and-views/share-of-search-the-new-most-important-metric-for-brands-google.

Plus, when a brand is on TV, many other digital channels share the wealth. For example, TV noticeably improves paid social media ROI by increasing both ad awareness and purchase intent.[34]

And digital supports TV in return. Paid search encourages consumers to respond after seeing a TV ad by placing your brand at the top of their search results. Retargeting visitors through digital channels helps them across the finish line to become a customer. And after an initial purchase, digital's level of engagement and personalization maintains customer relationships. But it's still TV that made the first introduction.

It's this type of strategic partnership between TV and digital that enhances performance by 50 percent.[35] When used to complement digital, TV reaches new audiences, draws consumers in, and reduces your reliance on Google to play fair. When used together, TV and digital boast a mutually beneficial relationship. Digital's downsides—overtargeting, increasing costs, brand safety perils, and fraudulent impressions—are alleviated by TV's ROI-boosting power, high consumer trust, and broad reach. These apparently opposing mediums mesh remarkably well.

Ultimately, television and digital both work toward the same goal: building your business. The key is to not get stuck on a single approach like Google did when they tried to tackle radio. Avoid their fate in radio by combining online and offline channels.

Launching an ad campaign on TV is a big move, and that can be intimidating. But to achieve big results, a big move is often exactly what's needed.

---

34   Mike Chapman, Matthew Fanno, and Craig MacDonald, "Television Turns the Channel on Brand ROI," Accenture Strategy, 2018, https://www.accenture.com/_acnmedia/pdf-77/accenture-television-turns-channel-brand-roi-accenture.pdf.

35   "Re-evaluating Media study shows TV and radio are strongest advertising media for brand-building in UK." Ebiquity Marketing, March 7, 2018, https://www.ebiquity.com/news-insights/research/re-evaluating-media-study-shows-tv-and-radio-are-strongest-advertising-media-for-brand-building-in-uk/.

Chapter 3

BANK ON BIG MOVES

POP QUIZ: APPLE. GOOGLE. TESLA. What do these companies have in common?

Besides being among the most well-known brands today, each of these companies has acted, well, outrageously. Think about it. In 1997, Steve Jobs slashed 70 percent of Apple's output to refocus on creating and marketing just four products. In 2006, Google spent $1.65 billion to buy YouTube—a price tag called extreme at the time of purchase—to expand their advertising program to include the largest video search engine.[36] And starting in 2008, Elon Musk drove Tesla to the top of the luxury electric vehicle market—a market many people claimed would never take off—with his strongest advertising being the image and experience of the cars alone.

This type of big move is far from uncommon among top brands. Microsoft introduced the Xbox even when it seemed nothing could

---

36   Victor Luckerson, "A Decade Ago, Google Bought YouTube—and It Was the Best Tech Deal Ever," The Ringer, October 10, 2016, https://www.theringer.com/2016/10/10/16042354/google-youtube-acquisition-10-years-tech-deals-69fdbe1c8a06.

compete with the PlayStation. Amazon's every other step has been unthinkable and unexpected, from prioritizing two-day shipping to launching its own line of perishable goods. Even TOMS makes the list for building an entire business model around donating half their products, generating intrinsic marketing attention.[37] Outrageous. But it certainly seems these bold decisions paid off.

Enduring and profitable companies seek growth, look for the next opportunity, and determine steps to rethink business models, transform operations, and even reinvent categories. Big moves mean big results. And aren't big results what every business wants?

In today's world, marketing is pressured by a need for major results. Advertising is exponentially more accountable as our lives have moved online. Long-term, executive-level marketers are expected to serve as growth partners for the C-suite, constantly driving the company to reach its full potential.[38] And as more brands trade their chief marketing officer for a chief growth officer or chief revenue officer, even job titles reflect the increasing importance of holding marketing teams accountable for revenue targets.[39]

Big moves mean big results. And aren't big results what every business wants?

---

37 John Rampton, "Businesses That took Huge Risks That Paid Off," Inc., October 11, 2016, https://www.inc.com/john-rampton/15-businesses-that-took-huge-risks-that-paid-off.html.

38 Nick Primola, "Why the CMO's future role is 'growth partner,' not marketer," WARC, April 15, 2020, https://www.warc.com/newsandopinion/opinion/why-the-cmos-future-role-is-growth-partner-not-marketer/3516.

39 Kristi Maynor, "You Can Take the M Out of CMO But Your Marketing Skills Remain Steadfast to a Changing Role," Forbes, September 30, 2019, https://www.forbes.com/sites/kristimaynor/2019/09/30/you-can-take-the-m-out-of-cmo-but-your-marketing-skills-remain-steadfast-to-a-changing-role/?sh=4a620c68236a.

But impactful and lasting growth doesn't come easily, and brands often get stuck trying to achieve it. We all recognize the need to move forward, but we're unsure how to do that. Too many businesses adjust incrementally while at the same time expecting exponential growth. But it typically doesn't work that way. Category leaders become leaders when they stand out from the crowd. People don't talk about a brand unless it gives them something noteworthy to talk about. Business-transforming outcomes require business-transforming moves—the types of moves made by the household names listed above.

Unfortunately, quarterly budgets, office politics, and a need for immediate results can all restrict your brand's ability to think big and be bold.[40] Companies that nurture a fear of failure often miss incredible opportunities. That dynamic begins with top-level leadership. If your C-suite isn't willing to try something new, different—and yes, maybe a little risky—the rest of your team certainly won't be. If your marketers anticipate punishment when anything goes wrong, why wouldn't they stick to small, incremental moves? Those moves are safe, easy, and accessible; they're low-hanging fruit requiring only mediocre commitment and middling resources.

It's true—you could slowly build your business one customer after another with a collection of small moves. But you'll eventually run into a roadblock. Besides that, worrying about a million baby steps that push you forward mere inches is a lot of worry and work for minimal rewards.

Digital advertising is a tempting solution for victims of this small-move mindset. Using digital alone, you aim to get out what you put in. You're relieved to report a definitive, instant response from

---

40   "Leading for the long term," McKinsey & Company, podcast transcript, June 15, 2018, https://www.mckinsey.com/business-functions/strategy-and-corporate-finance/our-insights/leading-for-the-long-term.

your ads. Establishing your marketing budget and company buy-in is simple because the data tells the story for you. You feel better about your job security, and leadership feels better about the company's marketing investment.

But with this approach, you'll experience mostly short-term effects. Just as quickly as those results appear, they'll be over. Because not only are returns on small moves minimal, they also will diminish over time. We explored some of these diminishing returns in chapter 2, including the decreasing effectiveness of display ads and significant percentage of fake digital advertising results.[41]

With small moves, it doesn't take much for your competitors to copy you. When everyone acts the same way, your efforts decrease in effectiveness until they're neutralized almost completely. Your business plateaus. And eventually, because no industry is truly static, your competitor gains an advantage. They take a bold leap into the unknown and are rewarded for it. Your incremental advancements can't keep up, and your brand falls behind.[42] Playing it safe with small moves just doesn't allow for long-term success in business.

And despite a constant focus on growth, most companies fail to demonstrate real commitment to doing what it takes to achieve that growth over the long term. There have been far too many brands devastated by shortsightedness, concerned only with seeing results now— even if those results are only the tip of the iceberg when it comes to what's possible. That's why prioritizing a balance between short-term performance and long-term brand success is essential. Only when you think long term and comprehend the bigger picture do you see the

---

41   Tim Hwang, *Subprime Attention Crisis: Advertising and the Time Bomb at the Heart of the Internet* (FSG Originals x Logic, Farrar, Straus and Giroux, 2020).

42   Chris Bradley, Martin Hirt, and Sven Smit, "Strategy to beat the odds," McKinsey & Company, February 13, 2018, https://www.mckinsey.com/business-functions/strategy-and-corporate-finance/our-insights/strategy-to-beat-the-odds.

types of big moves necessary to get where you want to go.

Achieving sustainable growth means leaning into a long-term strategy. The brands I mentioned at the start of this chapter weren't thinking, "What happens tomorrow?" when they made bold moves. They were looking much further down the line. Sometimes that means opening the door to risk. It means suppressing marketing's need for immediate results and being OK with stepping into the unknown by doing what's unfamiliar and unexpected. That's how you reach or stay at the top of your industry.

Thinking short term and small stakes is in fact the riskiest strategy of all. There's a much more reliable way to set your brand up for success. If you really want to shake up your industry and see dramatic growth, act like it. Take bold action. Invest in a big move that pushes you ahead of the competition.

Over the years, we've watched clients reap the rewards from their own bold moves. They've raised their stock prices. Gone public. Spun off a new brand. Advanced funding rounds. And there was one bold move they all made in common: TV.

> If you really want to shake up your industry and see dramatic growth, act like it. Take bold action. Invest in a big move that pushes you ahead of the competition.

BANK ON TV

Offering mass reach, high visibility, and an immersive brand experience, TV is the classic big marketing move. It beautifully balances your short- and long-term goals by driving sales response while building your brand.[43] It sets your business up for lasting success, clarifies messaging, and legitimizes your offering. It can also establish fame.

Just as many of America's largest celebrity personalities attained fame through TV, so have this country's biggest, most famous brands. And when your brand is famous, all bets are off. When you're able to capture consumer attention and create a sense of shared excitement around your brand, those big results are within reach.[44] Fame-driving campaigns outperform others when it comes to driving sales, growing your market share, building customer loyalty, and generating profit.[45]

Why do you think brands have continued to invest in Super Bowl commercials once a year, even as the cost of thirty seconds during the game has skyrocketed into the multiple millions for the media alone? The instant notoriety that comes from putting your brand in front of one of the largest and most diverse audiences possible in the United States is stunning.

It's this sort of dramatic investment that creates the momentum for wide-reaching, long-lasting brand impacts. First, brands that advertise during the Super Bowl do see sales impacts for months afterward, especially in markets that had high viewership of the game.[46] But the real goal behind many of these ads is to draw attention to the brand in a way that affects both sales and brand perception for the long term.

---

43   "The ten best charts from the work of Les Binet and Peter Field." EffWorks, March 7, 2018, https://www.effworks.co.uk/ten-best-charts-binet-field/.

44   "New brands must create fame," WARC, May 25, 2017, https://www.warc.com/newsandopinion/news/new-brands-must-create-fame/38721.

45   "The ten best charts from the work of Les Binet and Peter Field." EffWorks, March 7, 2018, https://www.effworks.co.uk/ten-best-charts-binet-field/.

46   "Are Super Bowl ads worth it? New research indicates sales benefits persist well into the year during 'March Madness,' MLB and NBA games" Informs, The Institute for Operations Research and the Management Sciences, January 5, 2018, https://www.informs.org/About-INFORMS/News-Room/Press-Releases/Are-Super-Bowl-ads-worth-it-New-research-indicates-sales-benefits-persist-well-into-the-year-during-March-Madness-MLB-and-NBA-games.

Major brands that regularly advertise during the Super Bowl, brands like Pepsi or Budweiser, have noticed spikes in sales in the weeks leading up to the game each year—even before their ad airs! Successful ads develop an association between the brand and the viewership of sports in general, so brands also see sales improve during other major games throughout the year. But for something like a single ad to have this much impact, it needs to be memorable. It needs to make noise.

That's why TV is the ideal channel for a dramatic move like advertising during the Super Bowl. Think about the potential within a fifteen-, thirty-, or sixty-second TV commercial to create and share content that's likely to catch on. TV's format allows for the very public sharing of your brand's story. That story can be emotional, provide some sort of practical value to the viewer, or even create a sense of prestige around your brand—all key elements to developing viral content.[47]

And the awareness TV creates doesn't just affect whether consumers purchase your product or service. TV helps brands attract new investors and partners. We had one client receive a call from Disney after airing on TV; Disney was interested in a partnership to promote one of their latest movies. The client gladly agreed.

Plus, the excitement around TV has an equally pronounced impact internally. Everyone from board members to employees to stakeholders feels the excitement when a brand launches TV. There's something about seeing your business flash across the silver screen that is completely unlike seeing a display ad for your brand online. It's visceral, compelling, and energizing.

We constantly experience the excitement shared by our clients. A CEO takes a picture when they see their advertisement on TV and emails it around the company. A group of employees sits down on an

---

47   Jonah Berger, *Contagious: Why Things Catch On* (Simon & Schuster, 2016).

airplane for a business trip and is surprised to see their commercial filling every screen on the plane. Clients report renewed energy from their sales force. One client even had distributors call to thank them for building their category's visibility.

> There's something about seeing your business flash across the silver screen that is completely unlike seeing a display ad for your brand online. It's visceral, compelling, and energizing.

That kind of energy trickles down into positive business benefits. When your employees are more excited about their work, their productivity improves.[48] One Gallup study found businesses with high levels of employee engagement are 22 percent more profitable than those with low levels.[49] Many of our clients even feature their own employees in their TV ads, creating another level of connection and pride.

And when you've made one big move, the doors open to countless other business-transforming ideas and directions. The ripple effects of launching TV reach all areas of a business, impacting brands in ways most could never imagine until it happens. Marketing Architects would know. Because in 2011, we became one of our own clients. And learned exactly what TV could accomplish.

---

48 Andrew J. Oswald, Eugenio Proto, and Daniel Sgroi, "Happiness and productivity," *Journal of Labor Economics* 33 (4), pp. 789-822, https://wrap.warwick.ac.uk/63228/7/WRAP_Oswald_681096.pdf.

49 Susan Sorenson, "How Employee Engagement Drives Growth," Gallup, June 20, 2013, https://www.gallup.com/workplace/236927/employee-engagement-drives-growth.aspx.

A GOOD IDEA GOES GOLDEN

We decided to create and sell our very own product. It would help us better understand the client experience from concept to market. Plus, it would give us a chance to use our own services to advertise a product in the way we believed was most effective.

Of course, in true Marketing Architects fashion, we steered clear of industries with a low barrier to entry. We weren't about to experiment with craft beers or scented candles. We were inspired to take on something with a higher purpose. These beliefs led us to the government-regulated medical device industry. We set out to reinvent the traditional walking cane.

We began with research—a lot of it. The standard cane hadn't seen real innovation in centuries. Surely, we could do better. We just needed to learn the traditional cane's failings. We began an extensive interview process with everyday cane users. The feedback? Traditional canes were bulky, an extra item to bring with you when mobility was already a challenge. This inspired a revolutionary idea. A cane shouldn't be another object to worry about. It should be an extension of the user's body. With that in mind, we built a cane designed to mimic a human's ankle and foot with a pivoting base. The cane expanded and retracted to best suit the individual user. It folded down to less than a third of its length for easy portability and storage—and unfolded automatically for immediate use.

But our history in advertising taught us we needed something else, something truly different, to help set the cane apart in a crowded industry.

That was when one of our creative directors walked into my office with a cane prototype. He placed the cane upright on my desk and asked, "Can we make it stand?" Intrigued, I said, "Well, I suppose so.

But why?" And he answered, "Because then it's the cane that stands alone." This was it. This was the solution to enable mobility on a level unmatched by the traditional cane.

We had the product. It was time to bring it to market. We created the branding—the name "HurryCane," inspired by a hurricane's unstoppable force. Because with this cane, there was no stopping the user. Then we prepared to launch TV advertising. We explored different creative strategies and adjusted the call to action so customers preferring to shop online could navigate to a URL rather than call a 1-800 number. Then, we launched.

Performance was fine. It was a successful campaign, but this was a cane unlike any other. We had developed a unique brand for what we thought was a groundbreaking product. We'd expected earth-shattering, headline-making results. But for that to happen, we needed to do more. Sometimes, discovering TV's full potential for your brand takes time spent iterating and testing.

That's when an unexpected opportunity arose.

When buying media, inventory occasionally becomes available at the last minute if an advertiser backs out. When networks sell these newly freed-up spaces, they offer them at a lower-than-typical price due to the short notice. And as we were evaluating HurryCane's TV campaign, ESPN asked if we'd be interested in a vacant space during one of its major games.

We hesitated. Even at a discounted price, the cost of the airing was significantly higher than our target range for HurryCane. But this could be our chance to acquaint a larger and more diverse audience with our product. Until now, we had focused our efforts on targeting networks and shows directed toward older audiences—the primary users of our product. But promoting our product to the general public watching the game would be interesting. It would give us reach and visibility unlike anything the HurryCane had seen. This was our opportunity to go big. We'd be taking a risk if we decided to air during the game, but the potential rewards of this bold move could change everything for the brand.

We agreed to the deal. HurryCane's commercial aired. And a longtime Marketing Architects hypothesis was proven—TV's broad reach has immense value. Suddenly we weren't only reaching the intended user of the HurryCane. Though the game's audience included a smaller number of older viewers, most people in a crowd know someone who uses or could use a cane. For example, many audience members were the children of our target customers. They faced concerns about aging parents' mobility and were eager to invest in new, innovative solutions to make their parents' lives better. People started talking. There was a new excitement around the brand.

Plus, airing on a high-profile network helped legitimize the product. Brands whose commercials air on major news networks or during big-time sporting events especially benefit from TV's instant credibility. And for a product in the medical device industry, trustworthiness was essential. The commercial created the momentum necessary for the product to truly take off. It was exactly the opportunity the HurryCane needed to make it onto the map.

We scaled into retail, and the HurryCane became a top seller at Walmart and on Amazon. It wasn't long before it was the best-selling cane in the United States. In 2015, we sold the HurryCane to Drive Medical, a medical device company with a diverse product portfolio and the resources to take the product even further. Today, the HurryCane is distributed on a global scale. And Drive still partners with Marketing Architects to use TV to spread the word about the brand.

It wasn't enough to create an outstanding product or to craft creative and memorable branding around it. None of that mattered if the right audience didn't know about the HurryCane. TV, used strategically, was the solution we needed to turn a big idea into big results.

THE BIRTH OF ALL-INCLUSIVE TV

Launching TV isn't a decision to make on a whim. It really is a big move, and that can be intimidating. TV requires buy-in from people across all levels and departments at your company. It usually means placing your brand in the hands of an agency and trusting them to handle it with the same care you would. And no, TV is not cheap. Pursuing it might mean reallocating dollars from preexisting marketing channels to create a TV budget.

But it's exactly this type of bold action that will create the results you're looking for. All big moves take courage. You won't get people talking about your brand by staying in your comfort zone.

However, just because TV is a high-impact marketing channel doesn't mean a test should induce sticker shock. A "big move" should be an educated risk, not an unthinkable one. There's a cost to any bold move, but if yours has you jeopardizing everything with little to no assurance of success, something's wrong.

> All big moves take courage. You won't get people talking about your brand by staying in your comfort zone.

Over the years, we've worked to de-risk TV for brands. We remembered a lesson from back in our days of selling only radio campaigns. Clients repeatedly hesitated to invest in producing multiple versions of their commercials. It was understandable. It was hard enough to justify paying for an untested venture without worrying about the steep price of producing more than one commercial. But that testing was exactly what was needed to prove whether the channel could work for the brand. We could take our best guess about creative direction, but nothing could beat actual consumer data telling us what people thought. And at that point, clients were only going to get that data if they invested in multiple swings. For many clients, that was too much commitment. They were toeing the line between small and big moves, frightened to truly take the plunge.

When one client had subpar campaign results, we suggested they try a new creative message. They refused because of a constricted budget. We said we'd cover the cost. This was unprecedented in the typical agency business, where high overhead costs and hourly billing are the norm. We saw it as an investment and a big move of our own. If their campaign performed better with this new creative, they would likely continue radio advertising and maintain our agency-client relationship. This would benefit everyone in the long run.

The client supplied the script. We produced the creative. And the new commercial dramatically outperformed their earlier version. It had simply taken a couple of tries to find the correct approach, reinforcing the importance of testing. Even with a clear success story, we knew it would still be a hard sell to convince other clients to pay for multiple creatives. So we decided to go all in.

Overturning our business model, we switched up our own approach to cover the cost of creative for all our clients. This gave us the freedom to make and test five or six creative versions to figure out the best option. When we were able to take the time and money needed to develop a top-performing commercial, we saw a better bottom-line result for our clients and for ourselves. And our clients were thrilled. They were able to get their brand on air for a fraction of the cost of working with our competitors.

As radio's effectiveness decreased and we moved into TV, we faced the same challenge in convincing clients to invest in everything they needed for a successful campaign. Brands hesitated to pay for extra services. And when they had to find a new partner to manage each area, the costs stacked up quickly. More partners led to less alignment and more finger pointing when things went wrong. But those "extra" pieces of a campaign were as essential for success as the creative and the media.

We expanded our model. We developed more services based on our experiences with what worked best. When clients had trouble measuring TV's results, we built our own attribution models. When consumer response was weak, we invested in conversion technology like chatbots to accelerate the sale. And when clients started to scale and needed sophisticated account planning, we brought in strategists and extensive consumer research tools.

We offered all these services at no additional cost to our clients, something unheard of in the agency business. And we named it All-Inclusive TV.

Our All-Inclusive model houses five platforms: strategy, media, creative, conversion, and analytics. Our clients are given full access to every platform for one price: the cost of media alone. With All-Inclusive TV, you no longer need millions of dollars for a quality TV test to see if the channel drives your necessary sales results. All-Inclusive TV makes TV advertising accessible for brands of many sizes and budgets. And it makes our job easier because we handle the entire TV campaign, soup to nuts. Decisions are streamlined. If something goes wrong, it's up to us to identify the problem and fix it.

Paying for these services was our own big move. This was our reinvention of television advertising, our redefinition of an entire category. We weren't just any old TV agency. We were the All-Inclusive TV agency.

Paying for all these services wasn't an altruistic move. It was a strategic one. If we were able to apply clients' TV budgets directly to media alone, they would grow to be larger businesses and larger clients, benefiting everyone in the end. Paying for TV services also meant we were doubly invested in discovering the most effective ways to create a successful campaign. But building each of our five platforms taught us more than how to do TV advertising right.

The chapters that follow will share strategies and best practices for TV. Even if your brand isn't on TV or you don't plan on testing the channel anytime soon, mastering the fundamentals of a successful TV campaign will give you tools to improve all your marketing efforts.

There's a reason so many people are impacted when you launch TV. Choosing creative messaging, targeting a profitable audience within a sea of media options, measuring effectiveness—it all requires alignment and expertise from every level of your company.

Success on TV takes a village. Most bold moves do.

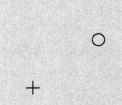

Part Two

HOW TO BUILD
WORLD-CLASS
TV CAMPAIGNS

Chapter 4

STRATEGY: CONSUMERS ARE CHANGING FASTER THAN COMPANIES

TEN DAYS. WE HAD JUST TEN DAYS from initial brand-agency conversation to launching a national TV campaign. And eight of those days sat between getting the official green light and getting on air. It was the fastest we had ever completed a campaign.

Such a quick turnaround is not typical in the TV industry. Normal timelines from concept to the small screen stretch across weeks or even months. But when a direct-to-consumer brand came to us amid a worldwide crisis and said they needed to be on TV immediately, we were ready for the challenge.

A family-run fresh-roasted nuts store, the Newark Nut Company, was founded in 1929, just as the stock market crash ushered in the Great Depression. Success through the worst economic downturn in recent history was possible because of the company's emphasis on top-quality produce and meticulous attention to perfecting the roasting process.

Three generations later, the Newark Nut Company continues to prioritize quality and service under the name Nuts.com. The company's breadth of products—they've always sold much more than nuts—sets them apart. On their site you can find dried fruits, baking goods, and snacks typically found at your local grocery store, but you can also find niche items like banana ketchup, dragon fruit powder, and vegan marshmallows. Nuts.com is the go-to site if you need five pounds of fresh chestnuts, ten pounds of popcorn, or every item that could possibly be used in a trail mix.

The transition to an e-commerce platform also allowed the brand to lean into convenience. On Nuts.com, you can order with a click of your mouse or a tap of your finger. The products will be shipped to your doorstep in brightly colored resealable bags, often arriving in just days. There's no additional errand to run, no physical store shelves to scour. Just a tidy navigation bar at the top of their website.

In the spring of 2020, the coronavirus pandemic and a faltering economy caused consumer behavior to shift at an accelerated pace. Consumers quickly found new ways to work, learn, and socialize while under lockdown in their homes. For many, the disruption of normal life also meant finding new ways to shop. Unable to visit their typical stores—many of which were experiencing a shortage of essential goods—consumers turned to e-commerce brands en masse. Online direct-to-consumer brands thrived. Their business model was suddenly envied by every major retailer. Plus, shoppers were prioritizing practical essentials like food and household goods. In order to stock their shelves with pantry basics without venturing outside, around 15 percent of US consumers tried grocery delivery for the first time.[50]

Nuts.com recognized they were in a unique position to provide both reassurance and much-needed quality pantry items on a national scale. Their business had long centered around providing products to customers' doorsteps without the hassle of visiting a store. Now their offering was especially relevant.

The problem they faced was spreading the word and doing so in the right way. At the time, Nuts.com's national aided brand awareness was only 6 percent. Nuts.com knew they could accomplish so much more if they connected their brand with a larger audience. That would require a big move.

With its mass reach, high visibility, and brand-building power, TV seemed the perfect solution. With TV, Nuts.com could reach a widespread national audience. As consumers relied more heavily on television for entertainment while stuck at home, viewership reached astounding highs. Plus, Nuts.com would benefit from TV's inherent credibility, which would be especially important during a time of great uncertainty.[51] And as big-name brands cut their advertising spend, media costs were quickly dropping. Brands launching TV could reach more people for less. If ever there was a time to be on TV, it was right then.

Nuts.com needed to get on air fast if they were going to capitalize on changing consumer behaviors and favorable media trends.

---

50   Tamara Charm et al., "Understanding and shaping consumer behavior in the next normal," McKinsey & Company, July 24, 2020, https://www.mckinsey.com/business-functions/marketing-and-sales/our-insights/understanding-and-shaping-consumer-behavior-in-the-next-normal.

51   Rebecca Stewart, "Advertising and social media face fresh trust issues amid global crisis," The Drum, May 15, 2020, https://www.thedrum.com/news/2020/05/15/advertising-and-social-media-face-fresh-trust-issues-amid-global-crisis.

The brand was perfectly primed to meet major consumer need. But even though online grocery orders were skyrocketing, and viewership continued to rise, no one knew how long any of it would last. The brand had to communicate its offering before the opportunity passed.

Nuts.com was ready to launch TV, and we were ready to help. We identified the target audience, the right frame of reference, and the messaging. Next, the team concepted and produced a commercial in record time. Our team worked long hours, but we met our deadline, proud of what we'd created: a commercial highlighting Nuts.com as a stress-free alternative to brick-and-mortar grocery stores.

The commercial aired. New and repeat customers flocked to Nuts.com, their purchases driving a positive return on ad spend throughout the length of the campaign. National aided awareness jumped from 6 percent to 16 percent in just two months. Created over the course of a week and during a time when countless major advertisers were cutting their TV advertising, the Nuts.com campaign was a resounding success.

We didn't want to stop there. Success in the short term is simple. Maintaining, and preferably growing, that success is much harder—which is why the right strategy is essential. Just because we made it to market in time for one trend didn't mean we could rest easy. If we knew one thing, it was that consumers don't stand still for long.

> Success in the short term is simple. Maintaining, and preferably growing, that success is much harder— which is why the right strategy is essential.

KEEPING PACE WITH CONSUMERS

You don't need me to tell you the world changes—a lot and sometimes quite rapidly. Consumers change right along with it. The modern consumer is more diverse, capricious, and tech savvy than ever before. And with the world only a click away, is it any wonder? Today's consumers have infinite information at their fingertips. They're more aware of sudden economic and marketplace changes, and they've learned to respond with their loyalty and dollars just as quickly.[52] We are in the age of the empowered consumer. Consumers call the shots. Brands and their marketing strategies battle to keep up.

The success or failure of any ad campaign begins with its strategy. Strategy is your battle plan. It powers your advertising from beginning to end by collecting customer insights, analyzing responses, and crafting messaging to reach the right customer at the right time. Your creative might be beautiful and your media well targeted, but if your messaging doesn't resonate with your audience or fails to align with your brand, you should expect only limited success.

Most businesses would agree with this claim. You'd be hard pressed to find a marketer who doesn't care about strategy. Most recognize the need to start off a new ad campaign correctly with a researched and thoughtful strategy. But in a marketplace that shifts constantly, a static strategy isn't enough. And it's here that advertisers are often caught, especially when it comes to a traditionally costly and slow-moving channel like TV.

Too many brands launch TV with a single, unyielding strategy based on one-time market research. They pay exorbitant up-front fees for a deep dive into third-party data exploring the state of their

---

52   Kasey Lobaugh, Bobby Stephens, and Jeff Simpson, "The consumer is changing, but perhaps not how you think," Deloitte Insights, May 29, 2019, https://www2.deloitte.com/us/en/insights/industry/retail-distribution/the-consumer-is-changing.html.

industry at that moment in time. This is important information, but it's only a snapshot of a much bigger and ever-changing picture. Focusing only on that moment would be like trying to guess the plot of a movie after watching just one scene. You'll likely discover a few correct themes, but there's too much room for error. It's difficult to make this snapshot of insight work for long-running campaigns.

It's honestly puzzling. We know consumers don't stand still—it's a core theme of the digital age. So why do brands look at strategy and research like a one-and-done task? Why do they expect consumers to freeze once the brand has established a direction?

One possible explanation revolves around TV's perception as a particularly inflexible channel. After all, what's the point of monitoring changing consumer behavior if you're unable to adjust your approach? Admittedly, traditional marketing's rigid reputation holds a grain of truth. Compared with digital, where campaigns can be instantly modified to better suit new trends, traditional offline channels are less responsive, with lengthy, expensive productions, layers of legal approvals, rigid media-buying timelines, and more.

But TV is more adaptable than many believe. Nuts.com proved launching TV doesn't have to be a long, fixed process. And we knew we could continue to evolve and update the Nuts.com campaign as we gained further insights through our strategy platform.

Strategy should be continually evolving and responding to the changing world. So we created a platform that could do just that.

Strategy IQ ("Insights Quantified") is the first of All-Inclusive TV's five platforms. After years of creating TV campaigns, we knew it wasn't enough to treat strategy as a "set it and forget it" service. Strategy should be continually evolving and responding to the changing world. So we created a platform that could do just that. It is through Strategy IQ that Marketing Architects TV campaigns are born, their messaging developed and audiences discovered—at no additional cost to our clients. The platform is part of our investment in clients' campaigns. We know strategy done right is essential for long-term TV success and staying at the front of consumer trends. It's necessary for your brand's ad messaging to remain relevant as consumers adapt. And it's vital to making your brand's TV investment worthwhile in the long run.

THE MAKING OF A SMART STRATEGY

Imagine your TV campaign as a sailboat heading out on a long journey. The environment around you—the wind, waves, and weather—shifts constantly. You can't merely point the sailboat in the right direction and hope for the best. Someone must repeatedly check and correct the boat's course, someone who understands both where they are at any given time and where they want to go. We believe that to successfully navigate that journey, any strong TV strategy should include three stages.

STAGE ONE. Setting your initial course requires determining your target destination. Before beginning any work, you must know what you hope to accomplish. You need an end goal. How will you judge success? During this stage of strategy development, you must determine your objectives. Any campaign needs an early direction in which to head.

Most brands are fairly comfortable with this stage of strategy. Here's where secondary market research and trend gathering can synthesize and fill any gaps in your existing knowledge. This information helps inform the goals you set, the problem you'd like to solve, or the consumer behavior you hope to change. With Strategy IQ, we see this phase of the planning culminate in a Performance Brief. Think of this document as your map. It helps you understand the general route of your journey, shows where other brands have gone before you, and provides broad recommendations for the best approach to getting where you want to go. Once this is done, you're ready for Stage Two of building your strategy.

STAGE TWO. Before you cast off, evaluate the range of tools at your disposal to help set a baseline. Conduct a brand study. Understand your current position in the eyes of consumers. Identify the best way to communicate your message to them to achieve the desired outcomes. Review and test various creative concepts. Then conduct a final check. Is your company internally prepared for this journey? If the answer's yes, then you're ready to launch. Once you've launched, it's finally time to move to Stage Three.

STAGE THREE. Now that you've determined your destination and have a plan for getting there, it's time to monitor your progress. It's here that countless advertisers miss golden opportunities. And it's here that consumers will eventually pull ahead if you're not careful. Audience viewing habits change. Your competitor launches its own campaign to eat up your market share. Be aware of these changes as they happen, or you will quickly find yourself dramatically off course.

Conduct a media audit to understand how the campaign is performing. Review your short-term performance metrics. Are you seeing the results you wanted? If not, why not? If so, can those results be improved? Can you optimize for a greater return? Should you introduce a new creative message or test different media intersections? This is how you keep up with consumers. This is how you adapt to our ever-changing world using TV.

This third phase of strategy development requires a few key elements built into your campaign and strategy capabilities. You can't change course if you don't have the tools or technology necessary to recognize exactly what environmental changes are taking place. For example, many major advertisers rely completely on brand campaigns. This works for many large brands, but it presents problems if you need more accountability. Campaigns intended to impact brand metrics alone are harder to measure and require patience to see the full impact. For many brands, this makes your third strategy stage exceptionally challenging. It's much easier to gauge changing trends and behaviors when you have some immediate and tangible data to evaluate.

That's exactly why we generally recommend a TV approach that blends both brand and performance. The performance aspect of your campaign will provide tangible signs of success, failure, or any significant movement in either direction. To achieve this, your commercial should include a unique call to action, whether that means asking the viewer to call a 1-800 number, visit a website, text with a chatbot, or even make a purchase. Those behaviors—the results of your ability to convince people who viewed your commercial to act—are the clearest indicator of your impact on the consumer.

Brand-focused campaigns rely heavily on attitudinal metrics to understand consumer effects. They ask viewers questions like "How do you feel about this brand?" or "How likely are you to purchase from this company?" These metrics can be highly informative and helpful for better understanding how the public sees your brand, but they also only tell you so much. Just because someone says they'd buy your products doesn't mean they actually will.

But if someone takes action to call a number or visit a website, their attitude has certainly been impacted—so much so that you've convinced them to do something about it! Behavioral data paints a more complete picture by providing tangible and determinate indicators of success. This way you can more easily quantify the impact of your TV investment. Many marketers wrongly believe they can only achieve this level of accountability with digital.

Of course, to see and review response, you need to use and understand first-party data. Third-party market reports may have pushed you in the right direction, but now first-party data can offer keen insights into who your customer is, when and where you're reaching them, and how they respond to different messaging—in real time. These insights can genuinely make or break your campaign.

It's amazing how underutilized first-party data still is. With more technology than ever helping us record and analyze this type of information, countless companies are sitting on a wealth of data without applying it to their decision-making. With this type of knowledge, you can then go back and ask, "How do we make it better?" First-party data should inform your media planning and buying. That way, you won't overlook customers or miss opportunities for growth. You'll be able to optimize and keep pace with consumers. And when your customers start moving toward a new trend, you'll be able to move with them.

Your initial direction is only the beginning. An agile approach to strategy means your campaign can become better and better as you remain on air, receive more data, and learn more about your customers and the world in which they live. That approach might even help identify new areas of opportunity.

SNACKING TAKES OVER

Nuts.com's original commercial spoke to a growing need for safety and convenience during uncertain times. But as the weeks and months wore on, consumers tired of pandemic-related messaging. They craved normalcy instead. The opportunity to avoid grocery store stress by ordering Nuts.com online was no longer the relevant message it had been that summer. So, we shifted gears and developed new creative highlighting real reviews from customers around the country. Now that Nuts.com had gained some attention, it was time we helped establish trust by sharing stories from people who knew and loved the brand.

We also developed different creative versions to match the season. Because of their category, Nuts.com experienced various seasonal trends—whether for fall weather or holiday festivities. Hazelnuts and pumpkin products gained peak popularity in the autumn, while baking ingredients were more often ordered in bulk as people approached the holidays. It seemed intuitive that we tweak the commercial to reflect these trends.

As these new creative versions aired, the strategy team continued gathering data on response. At first, reports of another audience segment were anecdotal. The team noticed reviews from customers who didn't fit the mold of the brand's target audience. To learn more, we dived into the data, looking closely at who was responding and when. The results were surprising.

Third-party research and brand studies had both pointed Nuts.com toward one distinct target audience: health-conscious women. If you search Nuts.com online, you'll discover countless food blogs from this audience dedicated to raving over Nuts.com, their products, and their packaging. These women care about nutrition and healthy eating and often use Nuts.com products as ingredients in more elaborate recipes.

But when analyzing data across tens of thousands of TV media intersections, our team noticed male-skewing networks performed on par with female ones. When web traffic spiked after a commercial aired during a hockey game, it confirmed our suspicions. Somehow it was hard to imagine our audience of thoughtful nutritionists all watching the hockey game—a typically male-skewed airing. We had discovered a new audience segment: male snackers. This group of Nuts.com fans ordered from Nuts.com for different reasons than our target audience. This customer was most attracted to the site's vast collection of snack items. Nuts.com trail mixes and popcorn were popular and convenient options, ordered to munch on while working from home or watching the game.

This was a strategy breakthrough we couldn't have achieved without our team of strategists and analysts continuing to monitor the Nuts.com campaign as it grew and gained traction with consumers. It wasn't something original market research could have told us. That initial research wasn't wrong—there was a major audience among health-conscious women buying pantry items. But it wasn't the full picture either. It was merely a starting point from which we could learn and evolve the campaign into something more relevant and more effective than ever. The Nuts.com audience grew as the brand gained notoriety through TV and consumers transitioned their lives into a new normal. The brand's audience wasn't the same as it had been just months before, and it was important for us to recognize and react to that change.

With a more complete understanding of the Nuts.com customer base, doors opened to exploring new media-buying opportunities. We could also intentionally shape our creative messaging and appeal to this important audience segment. Perhaps most importantly, we had proven the value of strategy's third and never-ending final stage: *adapting to new information.*

This type of situation was exactly why we built our entire strategy platform around the idea of monitoring the changing conditions of a client's marketplace and responding appropriately. It's why we can advise our clients not to abandon ship once they've established a course of direction. We know they'll get where they want to be more reliably and efficiently by maintaining enough flexibility within their TV campaigns to search out and take advantage of opportunities to adjust.

The consumer is constantly shifting, and it's important your brand shifts with them. You might discover opportunities you never would have dreamed of—and would otherwise have missed entirely.

Chapter 5

CREATIVE: REMARKABLE WORK SHOULD WORK REMARKABLY

HOW DO YOU DESIGN a new children's toy? How do you make it special, something that will stand out from the countless toys already on store shelves across the country?

This was the dilemma I was facing in 2011. Marketing Architects had developed several products by this time, including the HurryCane, the top-selling cane in America. But as a dad with young kids, I was curious to see whether there was an opportunity to expand into a more lighthearted category: children's toys.

We started with an idea to update the typical stuffed animal. What could be better than your standard plush toy? A stuffed animal with pockets, of course. With seven secret pockets, the stuffed animals could conveniently store other toys, blankets, and anything else a child would consider their "treasures." We called the product a Stuffie.

Next, our creative team took a swing at branding Stuffies. The product itself was fun, but how could we convince parents and kids alike to choose a Stuffie instead of a regular stuffed animal, a set of LEGO blocks, or any of the other endless children's toys on the market? Helping this product break away from the competition would depend largely on the story we crafted around it.

First, the Stuffie had to be a toy that children would want more than others. This was largely achieved through the design itself—there's something undeniably fun about filling all seven pockets on a Stuffie. But we knew we could do more, so we gave Stuffies their own individual characters, complete with names and personalities.

Next, we asked, "What about parents?" They were typically the real decision makers when it came to the purchase of a toy. What value did they gain when buying a Stuffie for their child? What would make them choose a Stuffie over other toys?

To address this, the creative team proposed the tagline "It's what's inside that counts." Not only did this positioning highlight the most unique feature of the Stuffie—the many pockets—but also it gave the brand a value system. Stuffies could now teach children the importance of appreciating a person's character, who they truly are inside, rather than basing their judgment on physical appearance alone.

Running with this new approach, we wrote and illustrated children's storybooks to be included in each Stuffies purchase. The books connected Stuffies characters to specific lessons. Francine the Unicorn taught the importance of believing in oneself. Sky the Giraffe demonstrated persistence. With these storybooks, Stuffies were both fun and wholesome. Plus, parents were included in the Stuffies experience when reading the storybook to their child—teaching them important life lessons along the way.

With the product and branding complete, it was time to launch the very first Stuffies TV campaign. We needed something attention grabbing and memorable. The team wrote a ridiculously catchy jingle: "How much stuff can you stuff in your Stuffie till your Stuffie's stuffed enough stuff!" I know, it's a tongue twister. Try saying that three times fast, and you'll see it's also impossible to forget. This was proven when, on the *Tonight Show with Jay Leno*, guests Jim Parsons and Maggie Elizabeth Jones repeated the Stuffies jingle while discussing popular children's toys. It's just that catchy.

The commercial was a success. Stuffies gained popularity, going on to be sold in fifty different retailers within the next year alone. But it was the creative around the Stuffie that made it more than a stuffed animal with pockets. The product had meaning and appeal that caused people to buy. Because of creative, we had real Stuffies fans.

By the time we reached 2013, Stuffies were still taking off. But as we approached another holiday season, we wondered if there was a new creative direction that would better attract our customers and ultimately improve sales. We played with a few ideas, but nothing stood out from the creative we'd already produced.

We turned our attention to thinking more about the Stuffies buyers. Who were our primary customers? The child who used the toy, of course, and the parent who made the purchase. Our current creative already targeted these two groups by highlighting the fun nature of the product and the values built into the brand. Was there another customer we might be missing?

As it turned out, there was. We had completely missed grandparents.

Success came down to understanding purchase motivators. What did the grandparent want? What reason could we give them to buy a Stuffie for their grandchild? The arguments to buy a Stuffie currently presented in our commercials were likely secondary motivators for the grandparent, but what might be that primary reason? What did they want most out of purchasing a toy for their grandchild?

To be the best grandparent ever, we concluded. To be loved and appreciated by their grandchild. And, as we approached the holidays, to make their grandchild's day. This insight was the breakthrough we needed.

We brainstormed, scripted, and produced a new commercial titled "Dear Grandma." The creative begins with children writing letters to their Grandma to thank her for their Stuffie. "You rock, Grandma!" the commercial says, adding, "I love my Stuffie" and "I can't wait for you to read me the storybook" before the minute is over.

We ran the commercial on Lifetime instead of Nickelodeon, Hallmark instead of the Cartoon Network—targeting shows with audiences skewing toward older generations. This creative version wasn't about reaching the kids and parents. This was specifically for grandparents.

Our bet on a new creative direction paid off. Sales skyrocketed that holiday season. Reviews poured in from grandparents who'd bought the Stuffies for their grandchild, saying, "It was the perfect gift," and "My grandson loved it."

The Stuffie was the same product it had always been. The same brand. We hadn't changed a thing about what the customer received in the end. We had simply adjusted our creative to better appeal to a specific Stuffies customer. We had thought about their purchase motivators and the end value they received. And we'd done our best to communicate that back to our audience.

When it comes down to it, your entire creative process should boil down to thinking like the customer. Try multiple approaches to determine just what hits home. Create something for *them*, not for your brand or your portfolio. It's both that simple and that difficult.

But the work is worth the effort. Having the right creative can make the difference between an average campaign and amazing victory. That's why it's so important to do creative right, to create remarkable work that also works remarkably.

But here we face every marketer's challenge: *How* do you develop creative that leads to worthwhile results? Understand your customer. It's what the creative team did when they developed the commercials for Stuffies. If you want people to buy from your business, you must ask, from the customer's perspective, "Why should I buy? What's in it for me?" Of course, as any marketer knows, that's more easily said than done.

> Having the right creative can make the difference between an average campaign and amazing victory.

KNOW THY CUSTOMER

What is the most important element of a brand?

If you answered, "A well-designed logo" or "A clever tagline," think again. Design and positioning alone do not make a brand. Customers do. You know this, but you may also have experienced how easy it is to forget the customer's centrality.

Customers validate your brand. Their purchases and reviews take your business from theory to reality. Their perceptions of your brand's image, personality, and mission matter more than any document listing your values or company purpose. In many ways, customers are the true brand builders, not marketers or agencies.

If there's one golden rule of marketing, it's "Know Thy Customer."

If there's one golden rule of marketing, it's "Know Thy Customer." The research on this topic—why it's so essential to understand your customers, to study and predict their behavior—is endless. Articles titled "Five Ways to Better Understand Your Customer," "The Importance of Meeting Your Customer Where They Are," and "Building a Consumer-Centric Brand in Three Foolproof Steps" fill my inbox and newsfeed daily. And with good reason. With all the information at the modern consumer's fingertips, communicating real value is essential for any brand looking to last. The problem with "Know thy customer"? It's difficult to do.

For one, you'll never know your customer as well as you'd like. It's hard to predict with certainty how consumers think, much less how they'll act (unless you're psychic, in which case you probably don't need this book to become a top-tier TV advertiser). For the nonclairvoyant among us, predicting consumer behavior is impossible without help. Even with all the consumer research in the world, you can never know with absolute confidence how viewers will receive a new commercial before they've seen it. That's what makes the process of investing thousands to millions of dollars in planning and producing creative for your venture into TV advertising more than a little risky.

Focus groups have long been the go-to solution for this troublesome dilemma. Sure, we can't peek into our customers' brains, but why can't they simply tell us what they're thinking? Originally created for this purpose, focus groups first helped find how to sell World War II to the American public. Later, they uncovered how to encourage baking-mix sales (add an egg to the step-by-step directions).[53] Unfortunately, focus groups also face growing controversy and criticism—for legitimate reasons.

One problem with this style of research is that we're learning more and more that customers aren't great communicators. Often, they don't know or fully understand why they do or don't buy something. And putting a bunch of strangers in a room together, offering them stale cookies, and then interrogating them for deep insights into their psyches is rarely as effective as we'd like. Even in situations in which participants accurately express their purchase motivators, this qualitative information—shared in the form of anecdotes and offhand comments—holds significantly more room for interpretive error than quantitative behavioral evidence. That's not to say this type of research isn't valuable. Well-conducted focus groups can provide keen and useful insights. But they can never definitively tell you how customers will respond. They can only really point toward one probability or another.

Even so, the discussion around knowing your customer remains consistently at the top of all marketers' minds. That's why it's surprising how many commercials exist for the sake of the beauty or inventiveness of their work rather than providing value to the viewer. A commercial may boast stunning visuals and a clever script. But does it teach consumers about the brand or motivate them to act? Too often, the answer is no. A commercial may be technically brilliant and still

---

53   Liza Featherstone, "Talk is cheap: the myth of the focus group," The Guardian, February 6, 2018, https://www.theguardian.com/news/2018/feb/06/talk-is-cheap-the-myth-of-the-focus-group.

fail to achieve advertising's primary goal: turning the consumer into a customer. Without someone buying into your brand or buying out your products, your business won't last long.

In the same way that a logo does not equal a brand, gorgeous creative and top-tier commercial production don't ensure a successful TV campaign. The infamous Pepsi ad from 2017 stands as just one example. Pepsi's in-house team created a commercial featuring Kendall Jenner as the leader of a group of protesters. The ad sparked immediate outrage for appearing tone deaf and awkward. Pepsi quickly pulled the ad and issued an apology, but the story will go down in history as an example of a brand failing to understand its customers on a massive scale.[54]

It's not always in-house teams missing the mark when it comes to knowing their customers. Hiring an agency also isn't foolproof. In fact, in a 2020 study released by Ipsos Canada, researchers compared what marketers think consumers do versus what consumers actually say they do. Marketers estimated time consumers spent going online, watching TV, using Instagram, and more. Three hundred marketing professionals dramatically overstated how much time consumers spend with media in every single measure; their estimates were regularly off by more than 100 percent.[55] Even experienced professionals fall into trouble when they are expected to predict what the consumer does.

Even if an agency or in-house team uncovers a valuable creative insight, there are often other forces at play that prevent brands from producing creative that truly resonates with their customers. Often,

54 Thomas Hobbs, "Pepsi's ad failure shows the importance of diversity and market research," Marketing Week, April 7, 2017, https://www.marketingweek.com/pepsi-scandal-prove-lack-diversity-house-work-flawed/.

55 Chris Powell, "There's a gulf between how consumers act, and how marketers think they act: Ipsos," The Message, November 17, 2020, https://the-message.ca/2020/11/17/theres-a-gulf-between-how-consumers-act-and-how-marketers-think-they-act-ipsos/.

the HiPPO, a.k.a. the "highest paid person's opinion," overturns a research-based direction for personal or political reasons.[56] We've worked with multiple brands that spend an inordinate amount of time and money on consumer research, only to choose an unproven direction they personally prefer.

Here's the thing: performance is the great equalizer. The customer always has the final say on whether a given creative approach was successful or a flop. They'll answer with their wallets.

GOOD CREATIVE CREATES CUSTOMERS

Creative is about more than pleasing executive-level leadership or rounding out a creative portfolio. It might involve those things, sure, but it should also be results focused. *Good creative creates customers.* Different types of commercials achieve these results in one of two ways.

BRAND FOCUS: In this type of commercial, one intends to improve brand awareness and value—think of a Coca-Cola ad featuring nothing but a polar bear enjoying a Coke. There's no immediate action for the viewer to take, other than to think, "That's right; Coke's pretty great." These ads anticipate action down the road. Let's say that viewer is at a convenience store a few weeks later. He wants to buy a soda. He scans the store, sees a bottle of Coke, and subconsciously remembers how the commercial made him feel. He pulls the bottle off the shelf.

PERFORMANCE FOCUS: The other type of commercial uses sales as a determiner of success and looks for a more immediate sales impact triggered by a call to action. When I discuss performance advertising

---

56 Bernard Marr, "Data-Driven Decision Making: Beware of the HIPPO Effect!" Forbes, October 26, 2017, https://www.forbes.com/sites/bernardmarr/2017/10/26/data-driven-decision-making-beware-of-the-hippo-effect/.

like this, many people picture infomercials from the 1980s. Marketers tense up in dread of the phrase "direct response"; the very thought of such a thing sends them hurrying to protect their brand image. But just because a commercial intends to improve web traffic or increase your average purchase amount doesn't mean it can't also be a stellar advertisement that promotes rather than degrades your brand. The key principle of performance advertising is accountability.

As we've discussed in previous chapters, digital's instant measurability is highlighting performance advertising in entirely new ways. Marketers have rediscovered the value of definitively knowing an ad's impact. The industry clearly loves tangible proof of why an ad is worth the time, money, and energy to create. So it's high time we moved past our worries about "performance marketing" when it comes to TV.

Almost all Marketing Architects ads are a blend of brand and performance. Brand-focused commercials can be incredibly valuable, but not every company is Coca-Cola. Not everyone can afford to wait months to see the effects of their TV campaign hit their business. A lot of brands need sales now simply to stay afloat, and big branded campaigns are often extra expensive. Our clients like to see tangible results *and* build their brand. Think about Stuffies. We wanted to build a beloved, memorable brand, but we also knew we couldn't continue investing in TV advertising if we didn't sell enough stuffed animals.

Regardless of whether your commercial is brand centric, performance focused, or a bit of both, you do need to measure *something*. TV advertising that doesn't intentionally drive some shift—whether in brand metrics or immediate customer action—well, that's mere indulgence. It doesn't matter how many awards a commercial wins if consumers don't take notice.

This is the challenge every creative professional faces. If you think of your campaign as a fishing expedition, you could be in the right place at the right time—but with the wrong bait, all the fish will swim right by. Perhaps the best bait is a trusted and familiar control, or perhaps it's something new and flashy. You never know for sure how the bait will work until you try it.

That's why you must get into the nitty-gritty details of making something to attract consumers to your brand in the first place. If good creative creates customers, how do you ensure your commercial does exactly that? When producing your next commercial, how can you know whether you've chosen the right approach or you're wasting every dollar? Is this knowledge even attainable when consumers are clearly more complex than traditional market research manages to illuminate?

At Marketing Architects, it isn't enough for us to create a commercial that's clever or catchy. We want to create a commercial that succeeds at driving sales while building the brand. And as we saw with Stuffies, there's always a possibility that one new creative could drive greater response and create more customers than another. How do we know which creative version that is without trying half a dozen options—an expensive and time-consuming endeavor?

CREATIVE THAT WINS

We've spent years building a platform that is predictive of creative success. It's called Creative ESP, our "Emotive Solutions Platform," and it's the second branch of All-Inclusive TV.

> At Marketing Architects, it isn't enough for us to create a commercial that's clever or catchy. We want to create a commercial that succeeds at driving sales while building the brand.

We might not be real psychics, but with Creative ESP helping us tap into consumers' emotions and read the unreadable, we're pretty darn close. Thanks to this platform, we know with more than 90 percent certainty which commercial will perform the best before it airs on TV.

Reading this, you might be skeptical. After all, we just established that there's no foolproof way to know the full extent of how consumers will react to a commercial until they see it. So how do we do it? To explain, let's walk through how we approach five typical steps in any TV creative process.

STEP 1: ALIGNMENT. This is the introduction to the brand for the creatives working on a campaign. In Step 1, there should be consistent and regular communication between the brand and the creative team as we review the insights gained through initial market research. We ensure everyone understands the campaign objectives so the creatives can think about the best ways to make the goals reality.

STEP 2: DEVELOPMENT. It's time to explore options. In Step 2, we determine and begin building out multiple possible directions for the campaign. It's always great to explore a wide variety of angles, because the best ideas happen when you open the door to all ideas. We might have to reel an idea back from the edge of complete craziness, but it's likely we'll discover something special through that process. Recently, one creative concept resulted in a cartoon nut riding a horse. And who knows—by the time you read this book, you might have even seen that commercial on TV!

After this exploration phase, we storyboard the best ideas to flesh out how they'll come to life. Storyboards show drawn or stock images depicting the commercial and illustrating the potential narrative.

STEP 3: VALIDATION. Working alongside the client, our experts narrow the storyboards to between five and seven favorite concepts and build out animatics—essentially, moving storyboards—for each one. These animatics show the frames of the commercial matched with the script and sound in order to give a more complete picture of what it would look like when produced.

Then comes a crucial piece. We pretest.

Our experience with Stuffies taught us there's always potential for something better. What if you could know what that better creative option was before paying to produce it? What if you could know the mind of your customer without relying on qualitative focus group results?

To be certain of the best creative approach, we need hard and fast consumer data. But that is impossible without consumers seeing the commercials themselves. And producing and airing multiple creatives to find the winner is expensive. We took this approach for years but always thought there had to be a better way to find a winning commercial without such high up-front costs.

Pretesting animatics with a target audience sample was our answer. That was how we could gain valuable first-party behavioral data telling us how consumers would respond to multiple creative versions. Our pretesting tool puts the animatics in front of consumers in a survey format and asks them questions about the

> What if you could know what that better creative option was before paying to produce it? What if you could know the mind of your customer without relying on qualitative focus group results?

different versions. Using proprietary data from our years in radio and television, plus top survey technology, we're able to determine success rates of different creatives at over 90 percent accuracy. This pretesting gives brands confidence to know they're making the most of their TV advertising. They know they made the right creative choice before their commercial even airs.

To be clear, we certainly didn't invent pretesting; a lot of agencies offer pretesting technology. But I like to think we did reinvent it to better serve our clients' unique needs using our own proprietary process and data.

STEP 4: PRODUCTION. Congrats—it's finally time to produce the winning creative. A team of world-class experts shoots and edits the winner. However, producing even one commercial can cost millions, with charges ranging from craft services to talent rights. We would know, since we cover the cost of creative as part of our All-Inclusive model, and we've seen the costs add up in unbelievable ways. Did you know it costs exponentially more to shoot on a yacht in open water rather than while it is docked? We do. Have you had to go purchase new pairs of pants for your crew when fires in California caused shoots to last much longer than expected? We have, and we know from experience that eleven days straight of delicious craft service catch up with you fast. Did you know that one celebrity spokesperson demanded thirty pairs of shoes for a shoot, even though we were only filming from the waist up? More demands followed, and that one-day shoot ended up racking up about $40,000 in wardrobe and makeup costs. This story? As they say: "Priceless."

Even after seeing every unexpected bill under the sun, we still invest in creative. When we cover these production costs, our clients can be confident they've chosen the best commercial, and there's nothing holding them back from pursuing that winning creative approach.

STEP 5: OPTIMIZATION. The testing doesn't stop after we launch. We'll continue adjusting variables like voice, music, and offer. We've seen big impacts on sales from something as small as including free shipping or a buy-one-get-one offer. We've discovered that a voice-over reading a website URL instead of only showing it onscreen dramatically increased web leads for one client.

We'll test these kinds of adjustments against the original commercial to see how response differs. Real-life consumer data continues to tell us when it's worth making a change or going in a new direction. That means your commercial only gets better.

The Stuffies story is just one example. We've repeatedly seen the power of great creative through the years. We've learned it's essential to make the most of your TV investment by producing creative that genuinely impacts the viewer. We know that means understanding your customer and testing as much as possible. Otherwise, you'll always be wondering if you could do better. And the answer is probably yes.

Chapter 6

PEOPLE ARE THE PROBLEM; AUTOMATION IS THE ANSWER

E-COMMERCE RETAILER LOVE YOUR MELON began as a class project. Inspired by the TOMS sell-one-donate-one business model, two friends approached their college entrepreneurship assignment with a similar idea. They wanted to build a brand to be both a successful business and an influential change agent for good. Designing their business around donating to nonprofits, the pair of classmates decided to direct their earnings toward organizations fighting childhood cancer. But to share their success, they first had to make a profit selling hats.

The very first Love Your Melon knit beanies were produced in Oregon with small loans from family and friends. The brand promised that for every hat sold, one would be donated, until they reached forty-five thousand hats donated—one for every child battling cancer in America.

They officially launched in 2012, and word of mouth quickly bolstered the brand. Customers loved the soft, 100 percent cotton knits and stylish designs. They also loved the brand's mission. It was an amazing feeling to know that by buying a product, you were contributing to something good.

After reaching their donation goal, the brand moved on to bigger things. Their new mission? Donating half their net profits to cancer research until they'd given $1 million to the cause. By the end of 2019, the brand had donated over $6.2 million and over 175,000 beanies.[57] That's when they expanded their product line to include blankets, headbands, and sweaters.

Locally, Love Your Melon achieved significant attention. Founded in Minneapolis, the brand's immediate community appreciated their entrepreneurial start and altruistic mission. The buzz created from the brand's loyal and passionate fan base spread the word organically, while a strong social media presence constituted much of their marketing focus.

But Love Your Melon was known less nationally. As they prepared for the 2019 holiday season, the brand's leadership wondered if there was a way to really go big in getting their name—and their cause—in front of a broader audience.

TV was the answer. A national campaign would skyrocket

57 Nicole Norfleet, "Love Your Melon launches first national TV ad campaign," Star Tribune, October 30, 2019, https://www.startribune.com/love-your-melon-launches-first-national-tv-ad-campaign/564104342/#:~:text=Minneapolis%2Dbased%20knit%20hat%20maker,mission%20to%20end%20childhood%20cancer.

awareness and share their mission with audiences across the country. TV was the opportunity for the growth the brand wanted. We were happy to help make that happen.

Marketing Architects pulled together a complete campaign in just weeks, working closely with the brand's leadership to align on a campaign direction, modify existing footage, and test various audio alternatives. We wanted to create a commercial that highlighted both product and purpose for holiday shoppers. "When is the last time a hat warmed your head and warmed your heart?" the spot asks.

Next it was time to develop the media plan. The brand was completely new to TV. They had never experimented with a mass-reach channel. We had to make sure we got the creative in front of the right people at the right time and at the best prices possible—not the easiest objective in a media marketplace that grows more complex every day.

MARKETPLACE MAYHEM

Media is complicated, and it's only growing more so. In chapter 1, we discussed the complexity of streaming and the challenges of navigating the expanding world of advanced TV. But before diving into the extensive list of streaming choices, there are countless options to explore in linear TV alone. From broadcast to syndication, cable, satellite, national, and local, the possibilities can be overwhelming.

Let's say you walk into an ice cream shop. Instead of a dozen ice cream flavors,

> Media is complicated, and it's only growing more so.

this shop has hundreds. You see the classic chocolate and vanilla right when you step through the door, but as you keep walking, the flavors become more specialized. Pineapple upside-down cake. Matcha green tea. By the time you reach the other end of the shop, you're exhausted. You can only name maybe ten flavors from memory. Plus, as you've been reviewing your options, the menu has changed! The shop's employees switched out a third of the flavors for new ones. And you haven't even had a chance yet to look over the toppings. Now there's a line of customers behind you, waiting impatiently for you to make your decision. Feeling the pressure to decide quickly, you panic. "Vanilla, please," you say to the worker.

Now imagine this same scenario with media. The overwhelming number of options makes it impossible to manually track all the thousands of media placements. That can have consequences, because when you're selecting media for a TV campaign, the stakes are much higher than when choosing an ice cream flavor. You're not just going to walk away with vanilla ice cream when you wanted rocky road. You're going to end up with a diminished ROI that could mean the difference between naming your campaign a success or chalking it up as an unfortunate failure.

To add to the difficulties, the industry also lacks any real systemization. Imagine an ice cream shop where the flavors aren't in any order but are simply scattered at random around the store. Some have labels on top of the container, others on the bottom. Others have no labels at all. Worse yet? Only some employees sell certain flavors. If you want mango and chocolate and cookie dough, you're going to have to buy from three different workers. Each flavor costs something different and comes in separate quantities. It's chaos.

It's the media buyer's job to find the best opportunities at the best prices, all at exactly the right time. But with so many options, how can a human—or any team of humans—do that job? They can't. This approach to media buying may have worked for the decades when there were a dozen television channels to choose from, but now it is a completely impractical technique for buying TV inventory.

What makes this especially true is that the TV industry remains totally unique in how it sells media. TV is not wired together through one platform like digital. There are many hundreds of owners of inventory and thousands of places for media buyers to go. The positives of this system include competitive pricing and more options for advertisers, but those positives come with complications.

Around 70 percent of TV inventory is typically sold to big brands in annual up-fronts—where a brand purchases a guaranteed amount of inventory for the year. That purchase is usually at a discounted price (think about how buying in bulk reduces your grocery bill) but also locks in the brand at those prices and airings. The other 30 percent of media is then brought to the scatter market. The scatter market is made up of networks that held inventory back from the up-fronts in order to sell it throughout the year instead. These airings are offered at higher prices but can be a solution for brands needing greater flexibility or wanting to add to their initial up-front plan. This inventory is also guaranteed to the buyer.[58]

The approach today is not too far removed from how TV inventory was sold in the 1950s. Admittedly, it worked for a long time. But today's world of constant change and digital flexibility is no longer conducive to this model, and brands and agencies alike are starting to take notice.

In the fall of 2020, brands were reeling from the economic impacts of the coronavirus pandemic, and they started to reevalu-

---

58   Steven Golus, "An Introduction to TV Advertising: The Upfronts," AdExchanger, July 9, 2020, https://www.adexchanger.com/tv-and-video/an-introduction-to-tv-advertising-the-upfronts/.

ate their media buys. Media sold in that year's up-fronts no longer claimed the same value. For example, a buy initially intended to air during a major sports game was far less desirable after sporting events were put on hold.[59] Advertisers wanted out of some of their deals, but the system was simply not equipped to deal with the tremendous need for flexibility.

Massive advertisers like Procter & Gamble began to speak out, feeling that they should be given an easier way out of their up-front deals, since no one expected the dramatic change that year had brought. Procter & Gamble joined an Association of National Advertisers task force with other major TV marketers and pushed for a move to a new TV buying schedule, improved research, and more transparency.[60] This push for change in the media industry is gaining more traction than ever before. However, most of that change has not happened yet—and will likely take some time to become the norm.

Where does this leave media buyers? It leaves them choosing vanilla from a smorgasbord of much more interesting opportunities. When the human brain is overwhelmed by choices, it defaults to what's known, and we simply can't analyze everything enough to feel confident placing bets on unknowns. When trying to sort through several hundred potential media placements, one tends to stick with what seems certain. If you're a buyer who bought and achieved success at some point in the past with six specific networks, you'll continue to buy those six. Maybe that's fine. Your clients might see some level

59   Phoebe Bain, "Advertisers Get Up Front with Networks about Upfronts," Marketing Brew, September 2, 2020, https://www.morningbrew.com/marketing/stories/2020/09/02/advertisers-get-front-networks-upfronts.

60   Wayne Friedman, "TV Upfront Disruption to Come: P&G Says Enough FOMO," Media Post, September 25, 2020, https://www.mediapost.com/publications/article/356240/tv-upfront-disruption-to-come-pg-says-enough-fom.html.

of consistent success. And you'll have developed strong relationships with those networks.

But missed opportunities can be devastating. Is it enough for your media rates to be average? Most brands can't afford to pay typical TV media rates *and* scale a campaign. Wouldn't you want the best rates on the right networks at the most opportune times? Defaulting to what appears to be the path of least resistance is a natural human reaction, but it's also one that can get in the way of the best possible outcomes.[61]

As I watched media evolve over the last couple of decades, I knew there was a better way to buy and sell inventory. Technology is the problem—creating too many media options for a human to track and evaluate thoroughly. But technology is also the solution: What if it wasn't a human doing that work?

> Technology is the problem—creating too many media options for a human to track and evaluate thoroughly. But technology is also the solution.

INTRODUCING ANNIKA

The third platform in our All-Inclusive TV model, Media AI², serves as our media-buying and optimization platform, and it is designed to solve typical media marketplace challenges by using automation and artificial intelligence. We dreamed of building a system

---

61   Hannah Gillett, "The question of bias in media planning," WARC, November 11, 2019, https://www.warc.com/newsandopinion/opinion/the-question-of-bias-in-media-planning/3296.

to battle the complex media landscape at an unprecedented speed. This dream resulted in technology so independently intelligent, we gave it a name.

Annika is the artificial intelligence at the heart of Media AI2. Annika leverages her superhuman processing power accessing first- and third-party data to present suggested-buy scenarios with greater accuracy and speed than any person or group of people. She sorts through the madness of the media marketplace to find the best buys at the best prices. Basically, she ensures you don't get vanilla ice cream except when you really do want vanilla.

Annika boasts the speed, precision, and decision-making power marketers expect in the digital space—but she applies these qualities to buying TV inventory. Here's how she works:

TARGETING. By now you know that at Marketing Architects, we love data. I've said it in earlier chapters, but I'll say it again: first-party data can make all the difference for your campaign, especially when it comes to deciding which audiences to target. That's exactly why we combine third-party research from sources like Kantar, Nielsen, and MRI with our clients' own data, like website visitors or online sales. Then we combine these with our own proprietary data warehouse built from two decades of buying media. That warehouse contains historical clearance, performance, and rate intelligence. All three data sources work together to find the best places to reach the right people at the right time.

We well know that those "right people" might be more than one single type of customer. Suppose your target audience is women who are interested in home improvement. Your media buys may include that home improvement–centric target market *plus* other female-skewing audiences. At Marketing Architects, we believe in broad reach over tight targeting.

Digital's supertargeting capabilities have the marketing world raving about personalization and one-to-one advertising. Every brand wants to spend their ad dollars where they'll reap the greatest reward. But we discussed the downsides of that type of targeting back in chapter 2. The more you target, the more likely you are to overpay, and the more likely you are to run into some faulty assumptions about who your audience really is, thereby ignoring valuable consumer groups.

Tight targeting with TV is a necessary by-product of overpaying for media. Let me break that statement down: when your cost per thousand is through the roof, you must limit your reach to only the best customers. There's no space for waste. Paradoxically, it's the most targeted buys that are the most expensive.

But if you're able to get a lower rate, there's some space in the budget for intentional waste. Because "waste" is rarely that.

TV is a social activity. People watch television with their families or friends. Even if viewed alone, TV often makes an impression worth talking about. Consumers mention over coffee the latest show they've been bingeing (and maybe an ad they saw). They buy or recommend products for their friends, family, and neighbors. These habits make your valuable audience much broader than one specific type of customer. If you can reach more people for a lower cost than that extremely targeted buy, why wouldn't you choose the broader option? Isn't that improving your chances of creating a customer?

Think of it like this: You're on a basketball court. It's you versus LeBron James, but there's a catch. LeBron has one shot. You have a hundred. Who's going to make more baskets? The answer's a layup.

Even business-to-business brands can find success on TV. Just because your customer or client is a specific high-level business executive doesn't mean that broad reach lacks value. Business purchase decisions are influenced by a wide range of people both within and beyond the company. That high-level executive you're targeting is likely to consider input—whether they realize it or not—from their neighbor, assistant, or partner in the decision-making process.

We've seen the proof of this phenomenon play out in our own work. One of our clients provides accounting and payroll software for businesses. That client found success on TV even though their customer is narrower than a typical direct-to-consumer brand's would be. Another business-to-business client competes in a crowded industry. Competitors spend millions every day bidding against one another for generic paid search keywords to make sales. Since launching TV, more customers are aware of our client's brand, so when those customers have a need, they go directly to the client's website or search for their name first. This rise in brand awareness allows the client to stand out from the competition and build an advantage for years to come.

DISTRIBUTION. Once we know who your valued audience is, we need to find the best places to reach them. Making the right selection from your massive media menu can quite literally double your campaign ROI.

Say you know your primary audience is sports-loving males. Typically, media buyers immediately jump to getting your commercial on ESPN. And Annika can do that, if it's the right decision. But we also know that because there are so many options on the media menu, there are often opportunities to reach the same audience at a lower cost. A major network like ESPN will be your most expensive option, so it's important to consider everything that's available before you pay a premium. ESPN is like that vanilla ice cream. It's the easiest solution, and it'll probably satisfy a sugar craving. Sometimes, it may even be exactly what you need, like in HurryCane's case. But when everyone else is choosing ESPN, there may also be cheaper options available. Annika does the math to weigh all your choices with the needs of the campaign to point to the best solution for your specific scenario.

The choices Annika weighs include the streaming side of the media universe, so you're sure to discover the best opportunities across the board. However, there remains a lot of potential (and cost savings) in the linear space. Based on the goals of many client campaigns, Annika generally recommends streaming as a supplement to linear.

MEASUREMENT. Once Annika has identified your audience and how to reach them, it's time to track and measure results. We've noted that TV advertising is tough to measure. That's why we have an entire platform (and an entire chapter of this book) dedicated to analytics. Annika's role in this process is essential.

Annika works with analytics models to evaluate and report performance on a daily, weekly, and monthly basis. This information is available to the client so they can monitor their campaign as it airs. We value this transparency, because we know our clients deserve to be in the loop on the status of their campaigns. And Annika makes transparency simple. With her help, when a campaign is performing well or poorly, clients don't have to take our word for it. They can see for themselves.[62]

PRICING. To help you fully understand how Annika works, I should explain her greatest advantage: finding the best media price possible.

In the spring of 2020, when the pandemic pushed major advertisers away from TV, inventory prices plummeted. US media ad costs declined an average of 3.4 percent.[63] With Annika's help, our clients

62 Carl Erik Kjærsgaard, "Why media buying and advertising is ripe for artificial intelligence," MarTech, November 18, 2016, https://martechtoday.com/media-buying-advertising-ripe-artificial-intelligence-192387.

63 Joe Mandese, "Report Projects 2020 Media Price Deflation: -0.9% Worldwide; -3.4% in the US," Media Post, October 5, 2020, https://www.mediapost.com/publications/article/356522/report-projects-2020-media-price-deflation-09.html.

saw a much more dramatic year-over-year savings of 42 percent. How is this possible? It's the power of our superhuman friend.

There's an incredible amount of unsold inventory left floating around in the market—usually at much lower rates. These can be quality media buys where advertisers have backed out, or it can be inventory that was simply never sold in the first place. It's out there. The only challenge is finding it. A human brain can't process all the information necessary to identify the needle in the haystack, especially considering the constant variability of the media marketplace.

Annika's artificial intelligence automatically evaluates thousands of media placements and predicts where valuable inventory lives. She allows us to make data-informed and timely buys to get the best deals when they happen. When one client came to us for help with their TV, Annika was able to reduce their media costs by 40 percent compared to what they spent with their previous agency.

Automation makes Annika ideal for our constantly shifting world. Annika was so successful in the spring of 2020, when the entire world was adjusting to a major change, because that's exactly how she's designed—to maximize efficiency by using the marketplace's variability for our clients' benefits. That's the power of technology today.

Of course, Annika is joined by a team of seasoned media buyers. Although the team is superhuman in my eyes, they can't beat a computer for sheer processing power and speed. Annika's automation and operational efficiency saved the team over a thousand hours of manual work in 2020. While Annika is doing what she does best, our team is freed to focus on other areas.

For example, our media buyers search out unique opportunities for extreme value in the marketplace. They focus on honing their negotiation skills to ensure the best deals. They're able to review and evaluate Annika's analysis rather than spending their working hours on nitty-gritty executional details.

And here at Marketing Architects, that's the way we like it. One of our company values is "Technology First." Technology's ability to streamline processes, expand opportunities, and ultimately elevate our work is incredible. So as a company, we prioritize tech. We've invested millions designing tech to help achieve the best results for our clients. Annika, the linchpin of our media optimization platform, was one such investment.

The greatest reason for putting technology first? By letting tech do what it does best, we free our employees to do what people do best. They can focus on discovering breakthrough media opportunities that help brands like Love Your Melon win on TV.

LOVE YOUR MEDIA

When Love Your Melon launched TV, Annika and the team put together an intelligent media buy that had the brand reaching audiences nationwide. This was a new endeavor. Love Your Melon had typically steered away from warm-weather states in the southern part of the country. This seemed sensible enough for a brand that primarily sold knit beanies designed to be worn in wintry weather common to the brand's native Minnesota. But the broad reach media opportunities Annika identified spanned the country, so that's where the commercial aired.

The results were better than planned. Love Your Melon quickly achieved a profitable return on their ad spend. They surpassed their sales goals. And they were stunned to discover performance in southern warm-weather states was on par with northern cold-weather ones. After all, "cold" is a relative term. Just because southern states weren't regularly facing negative temperatures and whiteout blizzards didn't mean it didn't get chilly now and then. And the feeling of buying a nice product while contributing to the fight against childhood cancer is powerful in every zip code.

Thanks to this media discovery, Love Your Melon had an open door to a larger geographic audience that hadn't been previously considered. Love Your Melon was now a nationally known brand. They weren't a local start-up any longer. The scale and quality of their advertising reflected the brand they had grown to become over the course of just five years.

Annika had made this possible. Love Your Melon could confidently try something new because there were multiple sources of data backing up every decision and artificial intelligence analyzing every outcome. Launching national TV was less of a risk and full of increased potential, because the entire media universe was up for grabs.

Annika makes sense of media's chaos. It's a job we're more than willing to leave to her superhuman mind. And we can rest easy knowing that as the world continues to change, Annika is continually adapting for better and better buys.

Chapter 7

CONVERSION: THE CONSUMER IS IN CONTROL

WHO WOULD HAVE THOUGHT Marketing Architects' next big opportunity would come in the form of a TV advertising veteran?

Our next client was a category-leading beauty brand that had been helping customers rediscover their confidence for years. But after decades of success, the brand noticed response to their ad campaigns slow. By 2016, the brand was intently exploring new growth opportunities. They decided to look for an agency that could help their business reach the next level by adapting to changing consumer viewership and buying behaviors.

We believed we could do exactly that. Annika crafted a media plan to tap unreached audiences, and we developed a new creative approach intended to better appeal to the brand's changing customer type. However, we still included the brand's traditional 1-800 number as the commercial's call to action—after all, the company had been driving customers from TV to the phone for years. But we wondered: Could a different conversion approach improve the campaign? Response should be simple and intuitive. And most importantly, it should lead to becoming a paying customer. Was the 1-800 number accomplishing that? Or was there a better option?

Because of the nature of our new client's offering, the time between gaining a lead and turning that lead into a customer could take weeks, even months. When a consumer called the 1-800 number listed at the end of a commercial, a customer service agent answered, gathered the lead's information, and walked them through their next steps. In some cases, a consultation would be scheduled, requiring the lead to show up to their appointment before they officially became a paying customer. Due to the time and increasing commitment between each step of the process, it could be a challenge to sustain engagement from first call to final appointment.

The complexity of turning leads into customers is hardly a unique challenge. In recent years, sales funnels have grown increasingly complex. Multiple marketing channels influence a shopper's decisions. The path from first contact to final purchase is becoming less straightforward, even for companies with comparatively short customer journeys. For example, online retailers consistently lose consumers between adding items to their cart and actually checking out.[64] And if too many leads are lost, it can completely devastate overall sales.

Unfortunately, some companies dismiss conversion concerns when approaching TV, thinking that if they create leads, they'll be

---

64   Revecka Jallad, "To Convert More Customers, Focus on Brand Awareness," Forbes, October 22, 2019, https://www.forbes.com/sites/forbesagencycouncil/2019/10/22/to-convert-more-customers-focus-on-brand-awareness/?sh=ed9d08d20759.

able to control the customer journey. That's simply not the case. As an agency with deep roots in direct response, we care about immediate ad performance. But we also know that it's one thing to get someone to respond to an ad, and it's another to make them a customer.

Today, convincing leads to take the leap to become paying customers requires more than a solid offering—even more than a great commercial. Brands need a strategic focus on conversion to make the most of their advertising and to ensure their offering gets the recognition it deserves. Conversion is too important to your campaign's success to be an afterthought. That's exactly why we invested over $50 million in developing conversion technology for our clients.

> Conversion is too important to your campaign's success to be an afterthought.

INVESTING IN CONVERSION

Conversion ROI ("Return on Interactions") is the fourth of our five platforms. It's designed to help you get the most out of your advertising, to guarantee technology never becomes the limiting factor in your campaign's success, and to ensure no lead is wasted.

In Marketing Architects' early days, we worked with several young start-up brands. They were innovative and exciting, but they didn't always have the infrastructure to support their ad campaign.

If we put together a commercial asking the consumer to visit a website URL and included a specific offer (perhaps 10 percent off the viewer's order), a consumer should see that same offer and terminology when they navigate to the website. This standardization eliminates confusion and helps establish a consistent customer experience. If the offers don't match, a potential customer may simply give up their search before digging any further into the site. But many clients didn't have the flexibility to change their website for each new offer—and their conversion suffered as a result.

The solution? We created our own landing pages where we could drive TV viewers. These pages could be incredibly simple or a replica of the client's entire website, depending on what the client preferred, but the messaging would match the custom offer shown in the commercial. We had the control and flexibility to quickly make changes as necessary or as one offer proved superior to another, without needing to go through the client's IT department or a third-party provider. That was one problem solved.

But another problem quickly arose. What about commercials asking viewers to call a 1-800 number? In those days, most of our clients partnered with call centers to receive TV-driven sales leads. But highly successful commercials driving record-breaking response could overwhelm the client's customer service agents trying to keep up with the calls. For that reason, we couldn't always push commercials—and results—as far as we knew they could go.

We repeatedly encountered similar challenges. One client simply wouldn't be operationally ready for a full-scale campaign. Another didn't have the resources to turn that many leads into customers. Unfortunately, this meant an advertising nightmare became reality— our strategy, creative, and media efforts were stunted. Our client could realize only a fraction of what was possible with TV.

But what if we could also offer a solution to conversion challenges? What if we could remove that barrier for TV success like we had with our drive-to-web clients? If we did, the campaigns we crafted would have more room for growth, and our clients would reap magnified benefits. If both our agency and our clients were spending the time carefully planning, crafting, and sharing world-class commercials, we could make the most of our efforts.

As an agency, we had partly gained our first advantage in radio by purchasing over twenty thousand phone numbers to use specifically with our commercials. Owning these numbers allowed us to track and manage the data behind them to help measure sales for our advertisers. By now, we were quite familiar with what worked (and what didn't) as far as 1-800 numbers were concerned. This was our comfort zone, so it seemed we had a strong starting point for addressing our clients' conversion challenges.

> If both our agency and our clients were spending the time carefully planning, crafting, and sharing world-class commercials, we could make the most of our efforts.

But solving the call center dilemma was a bigger issue than creating landing pages. It required more resources, so we invested in growing our team to focus on developing our technology capabilities. The result was an interactive voice response solution, a call center alternative we called Vocé.

At its most basic, Vocé was a sophisticated answering machine. The tech screened calls by differentiating between simple requests to be resolved with Vocé's preset options and others best addressed with a human response. We created Vocé with the intention of helping clients field more calls and make more sales. It could be used as little or as extensively as the client chose. Some clients used Vocé only for their call center's off-hours. Others replaced call centers entirely by preloading a script to walk the caller through a purchase. Most chose a middle path, using the technology as a gatekeeper.

With Você, clients could gain more leads without inundating their call centers. That allowed us, in turn, to take their ad campaigns as far as they could go. It was a win-win, for a while.

But the world was changing. Text was taking over everyday communications as more and more people adopted smartphones. Response to 1-800 numbers began to decline as consumer preference shifted. The shift toward texting caused consumers to anticipate immediate responses in their personal life. And it didn't take long before this also affected expectations for brands and businesses. Consumers were moving away from the 1-800 number, and we had to move with them. It was time to pivot. Our tech had to evolve.

Our next major investment was Abbot, an autonomous chatbot we developed in 2017. Like Você, the bot was designed as a call center replacement, but with a twist. Consumers no longer had to make a call. They could simply send a text. For some brands, text even had an advantage over drive-to-web campaigns by helping reduce paid search costs. It was the perfect complement to a TV campaign targeting the modern consumer.

Today, 88 percent of TV viewers watch television with a second screen in hand. They're already texting or scrolling online as commercials play, so why not meet them where they're at? Seventy-five percent of millennials would rather text than talk over the phone.[65] Why shouldn't this apply to how businesses interact with potential customers? Sixty-four percent of consumers now expect companies to respond and interact with them in real time, and a whopping 80

---

65   Ivana Vnučec, "Why Do People Rather Text Than Talk?" paldesk, accessed March 4, 2021, https://www.paldesk.com/why-do-people-rather-text-than-talk/.

percent of business-to-business customers expect the same.[66]

These stats aren't surprising. Businesses of all sizes have figured out texting's popularity. Even as you read this, you may receive an automated message from your dentist reminding you of an upcoming appointment or from your internet company providing a receipt for your latest bill. With text, there's no waiting on hold or unnecessary small talk. It's convenient and unintrusive, which we all appreciate, given our increasingly busy schedules.

Texting for businesses was still relatively unexplored territory in Abbot's early days of development. We wondered: Could we successfully apply the power of texting to more than basic customer service? Could our friendly chatbot be used in the sales process to convert more customers than was possible over the phone?

We were about to find out.

MEET ABBOT

Our beauty-brand client's advertising was ready for a conversion overhaul. The commercial we launched using a 1-800 number did see improved response, thanks to the updated creative and strategic media plan. But there was still untapped potential, an opportunity to bring the campaign to new heights. The brand recognized conversion could make all the difference, and they weren't about to overlook opportunities to improve. Could this client, a longtime master of the 1-800 number, drive TV viewers to respond via text?

We adjusted the creative to ask TV viewers to text the number shown on screen. "Text PROMO to 234234," one spot says, reminding viewers of a giveaway the brand was promoting. "Don't forget, that's

---

66 "State of the Connected Customer," Salesforce Research, accessed March 4, 2021, https://www.salesforce.com/content/dam/web/en_us/www/documents/e-books/state-of-the-connected-customer-report-second-edition2018.pdf.

P-R-O-M-O to 234234." Next, we prepared Abbot to answer text inquiries with a preloaded script guiding users from the first "Hello!" to scheduling a consult. Then we aired the commercial.

Leads increased by 400 percent. We were stunned. We had expected a boost in response, but this was even more than we had imagined. Adjusting the suggested mode of response made *that* much of a difference. But the increased response also revealed an important insight about our client's target audience. For many, discussing insecurities about their appearance over the phone was intimidating. But a text conversation with Abbot? Well, that was safe, private, and low risk. It was little wonder leads increased so much.

The next step was making sure those leads didn't drift off as we moved through the process from lead to customer. Increasing the number of leads wasn't enough if none of them converted. We believed Abbot could help with this too.

As more people responded to the commercials via text, Abbot gathered data on drop-off rates. Abbot learned where leads began to disconnect and where they quickly responded. Based on this data, Abbot's script was customized for optimal completion rates. If people were unlikely to share their email address after only two questions, Abbot could shift the request for an email address toward the end of the script. It was that simple.

Then we took it a step further. We incorporated the ability to schedule a consultation through a conversation with Abbot. Leads could see and select actual available consultation times at the nearest location. Then Abbot asked if they'd like to add the appointment to their calendar. Finally, leads could opt in for text reminders as the date neared. After our client added these features to their Abbot script, the number of scheduled appointments rose, as did the number of people who showed up for those appointments.

Abbot's built-in flexibility also proved helpful when COVID-19 put the brand's business on hold in the spring of 2020. Abbot had been designed to support nimble A/B testing to compare the impact of an alternative offer on conversion rates. This provides a simple way to ensure campaigns truly have the greatest possible impact and the flexibility to easily adjust the script. So when the world—and the consumer—changed drastically, our tech and our client kept up.

This is just one texting success story. Abbot has been a game changer for multiple clients. In fact, Abbot's conversion rate is so impressive that clients have worked to drive a greater percentage of their prospects to Abbot rather than other channels. One client saw Abbot could increase the likelihood a consumer would complete a traditional lead-generation form, so they replaced their mobile lead form with Abbot.

Campaigns that relied on Abbot found success because they were able to change as the world changed, and because the brands these campaigns represented were willing to move in a new direction. If our beauty-brand client had resisted trying something new, the company wouldn't have discovered a major opportunity. Just because 1-800 numbers had worked in the past didn't eliminate the possibility of there being a better option for the future.

DEPENDING ON THE CONSUMER

The shift from call to text isn't the final move. The consumer is still changing, and tech and conversion capabilities must do the same. Brands must be willing to invest in new technology—and to turn in new directions—in order to keep up with their customers. Our clients have done this when agreeing to drive viewers to text rather than 1-800 numbers. Marketing Architects did this when we moved our primary focus from Vocé to Abbot. But we're still constantly reevaluating ways to improve our conversion capabilities, including increasing personalization to provide recommendations based on a customer's previous purchase history.

Brands must be willing to invest in new technology—and to turn in new directions—in order to keep up with their customers.

Today many of our clients generate sales with drive-to-web campaigns, since more audiences have adopted the internet for shopping. However, others still find success with 1-800 numbers. Yet others are staunch Abbot advocates. Another client drives to web in their TV spot, but has Abbot launch from their website when the lead is on a mobile device, thereby streamlining the customer experience. There are plenty of options when it comes to conversion technology. The challenge becomes choosing which route is right for your campaign.

Decisions to adapt our technology or revise a conversion strategy all depend on how consumers already choose to respond. They have control, after all, in any campaign. And we've learned the best response method is different for each brand. The right approach depends on the target audience, which our strategy and conversion teams can help clients better understand.

For example, if your brand targets consumers over the age of sixty-five, you'll likely find better results using 1-800 numbers. If your brand targets millennials, you may discover more success driving to web or text. But age is just one variable of many impacting the ideal response method. It takes seasoned experts to evaluate these variables and recommend the best choice. It's why we've gathered a team that knows advertising, technology, and how consumers think.

Our conversion team consults with clients to analyze their unique situation and provide recommendations on everything from offer testing to tailored applications of our technology. They gather research and use their knowledge of your customer to determine the right solution. They find the answer to the question, "How does my consumer want to respond?" Then we adapt our tech capabilities to make that answer a reality. And then we test some more to make the solutions even better.

There's always room for improvement. In fact, that's one of my favorite things about the conversion side of any campaign—the sheer possibility, the continuous growth. From call routing to Abbot to custom URLs for unique and trackable landing pages, conversion technology has the capability to evolve with the consumer and to grow more advanced and insightful, whether that means comparing offers or tweaking messaging. Not taking advantage of those opportunities limits your campaign's potential. One offer might work well enough, but another may be even better. 1-800 numbers might be moderately successful, but texting could help your brand take off. You simply don't know until you try. And incremental improvements can add up to significant advances in the end.

We know we only win when our clients win and that our clients win when they acquire real, valuable customers. The right technology can go a long way toward getting those customers on board. And the right team can help you find and use that technology as effectively as possible. So don't neglect conversion. It should be an intentional piece of your campaign and is worth taking the time and resources to get right. Your customers—and your bottom line—will thank you.

Chapter 8

ANALYTICS: DATA GETS TWISTED EVERY DAMN DAY

HOME IMPROVEMENT COMPANY 1-800-HANSONS was a prominent advertiser in its home city of Detroit and other established markets. Campaigns relied on the brand's reputation as a trusted remodeler with three decades of experience helping homeowners replace their windows, roofing, and siding. Capitalizing on the brand's momentum, 1-800-HANSONS opened five new locations, in Denver, Salt Lake City, Des Moines, Omaha, and Sioux Falls. All they needed was the advertising to match their expansion, and TV's brand-building power paired perfectly with their campaign goals.

But introducing your brand to a new market is a big step, even for experienced advertisers. In their new locations, 1-800-HANSONS lacked the brand awareness and trust they normally claimed. They were a stranger to consumers. When their logo appeared onscreen, it wouldn't elicit the same familiarity among viewers. The brand had spent years building their reputation, but now, in many ways, it had to start that process all over again.

To be successful, 1-800-HANSONS needed TV. By expanding, they were making a major move they hoped would lead to major rewards. The company had high expectations for TV's success in boosting brand awareness and bringing in new customers; in other words, they needed to very clearly drive both short- and long-term results. As the brand took their TV advertising across the country, they wanted to incorporate analytics more thoroughly into their media buys. The challenges—and risks—were piling up. There were a lot of unknowns entering new markets. It only made sense, then, to partner with an agency that de-risked TV dramatically.

With our All-Inclusive model, Marketing Architects could alleviate concerns ranging from predicting how the creative would be received to getting the best media for the best price. When 1-800-HANSONS asked us to manage their TV in new markets, the media team crafted a plan targeting homeowners. We tested different types of media buys, moving beyond news and daytime talk shows to look for more ways to reach consumers. Annika even managed to beat their previous media buy, sharing the brand with new audiences at a lower cost. And after proving our buying power, 1-800-HANSONS asked that we also manage TV in their established markets.

We realized their campaign still faced a unique challenge. The brand's commercial asked viewers to respond via a 1-800 number. Their name is 1-800-HANSONS, after all. Directing consumers to the phone had been a tried-and-true conversion technique for the brand for years, and it continued to drive response in all markets. But we also knew that just because we asked viewers to respond via the phone didn't mean everyone would do that. Many leads simply navigated to the brand's website instead of calling.

From a conversion perspective, that was fine. Leads that called the number and those that went online both were becoming customers. But from a TV attribution perspective, this divergence in the way customers responded presented a challenge.

If we only measured campaign success based on the number of calls, we would miss large groups of customers who went online after seeing the commercial. Call-volume data wouldn't tell the whole story of TV's performance. And without that bigger picture, we would fail to account for TV's true impact. We risked being unable to accurately judge between a successful campaign and a failure. And that is perhaps the worst TV advertising nightmare of all: investing in a campaign only to have no idea whether it worked.

> That is perhaps the worst TV advertising nightmare of all: investing in a campaign only to have no idea whether it worked.

THE DATA PROBLEM

Long gone are the days of making business choices based on gut feelings or intuition alone. What marketer or business leader doesn't love a decision supported by tangible and deterministic evidence? Unsurprisingly, organizations with a high focus on data are three times more likely to find positive improvements in their decision-making processes than those that are less data driven.[67] But for data to serve as the helpful tool it's meant to be, it must be collected and applied cautiously. Intentionally. Especially when it comes to TV attribution.

Let's say you just launched your first TV campaign. What is the primary goal of your advertising? You want results, right? You want to know that TV worked, that it accomplished what you hoped it would. If it didn't work, you want to know why, to be able to identify what went wrong and how to improve.

In theory, this seems simple enough. You established campaign goals when building your strategy, and you've been working to achieve those goals by optimizing your creative, media, and conversion. Now all you need to do is evaluate how well you met those goals based on campaign results. Unfortunately, the execution of this concept is where things become tricky.

Think about analyzing TV performance like you're putting together a massive jigsaw puzzle. You're surrounded by heaps of unsorted puzzle pieces. The goal is to put together enough of the puzzle that the picture becomes clear. It doesn't have to be perfect, just discernible. Of course, your challenge is made more difficult because some of the pieces are damaged—chipped or faded. Others have been painted over, showing an image contrary to the one you're trying to assemble. Some pieces are delivered to you at different points in time. Others are never delivered at all. Still others are from another puzzle entirely, throwing you off track.

The data points for TV are like those puzzle pieces; each piece tells you a little bit more about campaign performance. But like those

---

67 Tim Stobierski, "The Advantages of Data-Driven Decision-Making," Harvard Business School Online, August 26, 2019, https://online.hbs.edu/blog/post/data-driven-decision-making.

damaged or misleading puzzle pieces, data is tricky—and more problematic than anyone likes to admit.

First, too much of the data collected by businesses is no good from the very start. It may include errors or simply be outdated. In 2016, IBM estimated poor-quality data costs the United States $3.1 trillion each year.[68] Ouch. When your data is bad, it doesn't matter how skillfully you sift through the numbers for deep insights. Any conclusions are based on faulty information. All that analytical work is a waste of time.

For example, brands and agencies relying on old-school traditional reporting methods may wait weeks to receive airing details from networks. You may discover airings on one network performed poorly, only for it to be too late to do anything about it. You've missed the opportunity to improve your ad spend effectiveness. By the time you receive that data, its value is significantly diminished.

Even when you do have accurate and timely data, how do you know you're interpreting and applying it correctly? Failing to do so can have serious consequences. Another study, for example, found that 95 percent of business executives admit that misinterpreting big data risks major business problems, a conclusion none of us should find particularly shocking.[69] Just because you have all these numbers at your fingertips doesn't guarantee success. In fact, misreading those numbers can actually lead to disaster.

For most brands, the problem with TV attribution isn't a lack of data, even high-quality data. Our world is flooded by numbers and

---

68   Thomas C. Redman, "Bad Data Costs the US $3 Trillion Per Year," Harvard Business Review, September 22, 2016, https://hbr.org/2016/09/bad-data-costs-the-u-s-3-trillion-per-year.

69   Vladimir Fedak, "Big Data misuse can break your business," towards data science, March 16, 2018, https://towardsdatascience.com/big-data-misuse-can-break-your-business-ef6432dfd188.

information, and the TV industry has worked hard to get on board. As technology has evolved, so has our ability to track campaigns by measuring everything from web lift to new customers. Where many advertisers struggle is reading and sorting through these numbers to find meaningful insights and to apply information correctly. Your TV performance data can and should change the trajectory of your advertising strategy. But when incorrect or faulty conclusions are drawn, it's all too easy to turn your campaign in the wrong direction, ultimately harming performance and your ROI.

Consider one issue with measuring TV performance known as a "last-click-attribution" mindset.[70] Just because a lead clicked on a paid search ad before making a purchase doesn't necessarily mean paid search is fully responsible for that new customer. We've discussed this type of scenario before: unknown to you, that customer saw your brand's commercial on TV the week before. Then it showed up on their TV again that morning, finally convincing them to buy. They typed your brand into a search engine and clicked on that first ad that popped up. Often, that customer would simply be named a result of paid search. But that's only a piece of the story. Not accounting for TV's effect across the entirety of the sales funnel provides only a narrow view of both the customer experience and TV's true impact.

This situation is exactly why having data and knowing how it should inform your business decisions are two entirely separate things. A business with this last-click-attribution mindset and limited understanding of TV's big-picture effects may now decide to invest more marketing dollars in paid search, since that's what appears to be working so well. To compensate for this increase, they pull from

---

70   Dan Aversano, "Rethinking TV Attribution: The Full-Funnel Approach," Ad Age, April 18, 2019, https://adage.com/article/warnermedia/rethinking-tv-attribution-full-funnel-approach/2163991.

their TV budget. But since TV played such a major role in getting customers to those paid search ads in the first place, those ads are now less effective without TV. That's an unfortunate but common scenario for brands struggling to measure TV performance.

I'll admit it: TV attribution is hard. Verifying and interpreting TV campaign data is challenging. There's so much information—some helpful, some not—and it's all only individual snapshots that compose a bigger picture. How do you ensure you're seeing that larger image? How do you know when to attribute a customer to TV and when it rightfully belongs to paid search?

How do you know TV's true impact on your business within minutes, days, and months of launching a campaign?

Fears of inaccurately measuring the impacts of a campaign have more than once deterred a brand from trying TV at all. Measuring TV seems very fluffy and intangible, especially when compared to digital's definitive results. From the outside, TV attribution doesn't seem to have the deterministic accountability modern marketers want when making a case for their budget at year end. All the work that goes into creating a great campaign—from strategy to creative to media to conversion—only does so much good if we don't know whether any of it worked.

How do you know TV's true impact on your business within minutes, days, and months of launching a campaign?

Just because TV attribution is difficult doesn't mean it's impossible. There are ways to accurately measure both slight and massive campaign impacts, to see what's happening behind the scenes. When you have the correct systems in place to determine your campaign's value, the effort of launching TV is more than worthwhile. But that's also the thing: you really, really need those correct systems.

A MULTIMODEL SOLUTION

The critics are right, in a sense, when they say that TV attribution is often wrong. A better description would be that all TV attribution methods are limited, only showing a few pieces of a much larger puzzle. But if one method of understanding performance can help us piece together one corner of the puzzle, and another can connect to the center, and so on, we can start to build out the full picture. It's then that we have a much clearer idea of TV's true impact, from sales response to long-term brand and business growth. With this in mind, we decided to develop our own analytics solution.

Our All-Inclusive TV model rounds out its capabilities with Analytics DNA ("Data-iNspired Action"). We know that when measuring TV performance, there is no single, simple answer. No silver bullet. Sometimes data is bad. Sometimes attribution is wrong. But there are many partially correct answers that can piece together a more complete story. At Marketing Architects, we landed on the most accurate understanding of TV performance when we looked at it from multiple angles and considered more than one type of TV impact.

MICRO IMPACTS. The first of our models begins by looking at TV's most obvious and immediate effects. It measures small and extremely deterministic metrics. We use our own Micro Attribution Platform (MAP) to determine in-market creative performance, tracking response through a change in the number of calls, texts, or web traffic your brand experiences after launching TV.

Then our team ties specific media intersections to response levels. We look at how much you spent on each airing or each network and compare it with the response volume. We can get as granular as determining the response seen in the first six minutes after a specific airing on a specific network. Finally, working with Annika and the media team, we optimize your media plan for the greatest response at the lowest cost. We get that data in time to make real, informed decisions that allow you to take action to improve your campaign.

MACRO IMPACTS. Looking at the immediate impact alone misses other secondary factors, especially because not everyone responds instantly after seeing an ad on TV. It might take a few weeks, or a viewer might have to see your ad twice, before that person searches online or texts a number for more information. But once you've been on air for a while—two to six months is our general estimate, depending on the size of your business—you'll see other changes take place.

Your website traffic composition may shift. Online, TV primarily drives paid search, direct, and organic traffic. So if a TV campaign is bringing in customers, you should expect a greater percentage of your traffic coming from these sources. And as the weeks go on, you'd anticipate seeing your total number of new customers grow. That's a result of TV's broad reach at work, connecting you with new, fresh audiences who may have been unfamiliar with your brand before.

We'd also expect to see conversion rates change. The customer coming from TV saw your commercial and took the time and energy to search for your business online. They've already committed on some level to at least giving your brand a chance. This is no accidental click from a paid search or social media ad. Their actions show real intent, and brands find these customers are more likely to buy and more likely to buy *more*. One client found that even without increasing their overall number of customers, their business took off after launching TV simply because each customer from TV made larger orders.

BUSINESS IMPACTS. Some of the most exciting effects of TV are the long-term business impacts. Since TV should increase your brand's familiarity and memorability over time, we work with the strategy team and your company to determine shifts in brand recall. Likewise, you may discover newly opened doors, created by TV's credibility-boosting ability, for fundraising and investment opportunities.

I've even watched brands grow their pricing power because of their TV campaigns. One client saw their customer volume increase so quickly just months after launching TV that they could raise their prices. And, of course, revenue growth is most important to every brand with which we've ever worked. It's the whole reason to advertise on TV in the first place. That's where we all want to see change in both the short and long term.

Tracking each of these TV-driven effects—micro, macro, and business—we're able to see the bigger picture. We can gather multiple types of data and begin piecing together that puzzle. This helps ensure that we're working with quality information and that the big picture is an accurate reflection of campaign performance. By layering these models over each other, we can begin to sift out what's truly accurate. But just as important, we work hard to make sure that information is interpreted correctly and objectively. For that to happen, we emphasize data transparency.

> We work hard to make sure that information is interpreted correctly and objectively. For that to happen, we emphasize data transparency.

THE NEED FOR TRANSPARENCY

"They're a black box."

This is a phrase I've heard describe TV agencies many times over the years, especially when it comes to analytics. With "black-box" agencies, data might as well be stored in a vault. Attribution models and methods are explained only vaguely, leaving advertisers in the dark when it comes to their campaign performance.

There are two reasons this method does not work in our age of data abundance. First, an advertiser loses the chance to fully understand what works for their brand on TV. Whether your campaign is doing well or not, isn't it valuable to know why? That's something you're only going to learn if you dive into that information—ideally working with your agency. Second, locking away campaign data can naturally make an advertiser nervous. They lose control over ensuring that information is objectively interpreted. How is the client to know their agency is applying data correctly if they're unable to see it for themselves? It's like having all those pieces of the puzzle finally put in place and then being told you're not allowed to look at the resulting image.

The TV industry has taken great strides addressing these concerns in the past few years. As an agency with years of experience, Marketing Architects has the opportunity to walk alongside clients as true partners, providing education and hard-won insights. And as an industry, we need to be accountable to the advertisers who trust us not only with their marketing dollars, but also with their brand images and business decisions. Building that trust requires doing away with the old-school "black-box" approach. That's why, at Marketing Architects, we don't ask you to take our word for your campaign's performance.

We customize a platform for each client to act as a hub for all campaign information, from past creative versions to brainstorming sessions and future objectives. This is where you'll also find your campaign data, available for viewing at all times. Airing details and other practical pieces of information are updated in nearly real time. That way, you get the data we're collecting with our multiple attribution models *while it's still relevant.*

We make all this data available so that you have access to that full picture we're building of TV's overall performance. We partner with a third party to audit the information, and we also encourage clients to run their own analytics to cross-check the data we've collected. We do all this to ensure as much objectivity and accuracy as possible. We want to ensure that data doesn't get twisted, even unintentionally. And we want to raise advertiser confidence in the conclusions drawn about their campaign. Our ultimate goal is that clients have all the information needed to make the best decisions for their business.

Of course, transparency shouldn't be the limit of what an agency offers. We also believe in high levels of collaboration between client and agency. At Marketing Architects, we know TV advertising. Our experienced team of analysts is an important piece of that expertise, using knowledge to sort through campaign data and explain information clearly and accurately. We also recognize that the advertiser is the expert on their brand and business. When we put those two powerhouses of knowledge together, we can build something great. We can work creatively to develop custom solutions that make sense for your brand and your campaign. Once again, it comes down to our business model: we only win when you win.

A BETTER PERSPECTIVE

We were trying to help 1-800-HANSONS win. For that to happen, they needed to know TV's true impact on their business. That meant we needed to look at their campaign from another angle. We were counting customers who called the 1-800 number shown in the commercial, but what about viewers who went straight to the website?

Using Abbot, we built out a survey for the company's online lead form asking users to share how they learned about the brand. Suddenly, we had a whole new source of information illuminating TV's effect on web conversions. And what this information told us was astounding.

Survey data from the lead form showed TV's halo effect was five times greater than the phone calls alone suggested. This also meant that the cost of each TV-attributed lead was only a fifth of what had been initially calculated. We had known TV was bringing in customers both online and through the phone, but now we could see TV's impact was significantly greater than we realized.

And the short-term impact of new customers wasn't the only good news. 1-800-HANSONS had launched TV not only to drive customer growth, but also to raise brand awareness. After two years of airing on TV, aided awareness in each new market had grown over 20 percent, while the awareness of 1-800-HANSONS competitors had remained stagnant. We were able to discover this only by approaching TV's effects from more than one angle. If we had looked only at the micro impacts, we would have missed this additional piece of our TV performance puzzle.

The more pieces, the better. The more you understand your campaign's performance, the better prepared you are to make informed business decisions.

Any brand launching TV needs timely and relevant data that contributes to understanding performance's bigger picture and an agency-client partnership in place to use that data well. When you have that, you'll be able to make the most of your TV investment. That's when you'll truly be set up for success.

Conclusion

I'M SITTING ON THE COUCH AT HOME. Football plays on the TV—the Packers versus the Vikings. For any midwesterner, it's one of the biggest games of the season. But the kids are home, fighting for control of the remote and flipping through channels.

"Wait," I say. The channel surfing pauses. And there it is: a Marketing Architects–created commercial for one of our newest clients.

Even after years in the industry, there's something undeniably exciting about seeing a client's commercial on TV, knowing the many hours of research, planning, and analyzing that went into this single thirty-second airing. It's rewarding to experience the product of all that work from countless people and departments.

My years watching the teams at Marketing Architects help businesses launch TV taught me that the best campaigns require more than a clever media plan or quality creative, more than an adaptable campaign strategy, more even than advanced conversion technology or data-driven insights designed to propel a campaign forward. The best TV campaigns require all these things. Strategy, creative, media, conversion, and analytics are each essential factors for TV success.

To develop a campaign that boasts the best in each of those areas, you need a team of wildly different people, all experts in their own fields. My favorite aspect of TV is its uniting force, its ability to weave together all that knowledge and insight.

> Strategy, creative, media, conversion, and analytics are each essential factors for TV success.

All-Inclusive TV brings our Marketing Architects team together in pursuit of a common goal: your brand's growth. Thanks to TV, I get to spend my days with a variety of brilliant brand strategists and award-winning producers, data analysts, and account managers who constantly challenge each other to grow and think creatively, to innovate and improve.

TV also brings your team together.

When you set a goal as big as launching TV, you need support from departments ranging from marketing to finance. A major initiative like this unites these teams out of necessity. Clients have repeatedly reported renewed energy within their workforce after launching a campaign. That makes sense. A big move like TV? That's exciting. What could be better than watching your efforts come to life onscreen?

Plus, TV brings your customers together.

Advertising is often experienced by consumers when they are alone. Consider a paid search ad, clicked on by a single person. Even social media, for all its opportunities to connect online, lacks in-person connections. TV is different.

More than any other marketing channel, TV is the one we experience together. In 2019, almost half of video viewership took place in a group. And the social side of TV is actually growing. Forty-nine percent of survey respondents said they watch TV with others more than they did just three years ago.[71] My family and I gathering to watch the game on a Sunday afternoon is but one example of a much larger trend. I believe that shared experience is part of what makes TV advertising so powerful. That ability to discuss your experience in real time makes commercials infinitely more impactful. And finally, a well-designed TV campaign also unites your brand and consumers. That's really what it's all about, after all.

Part of why I enjoy seeing a client's commercial on TV is because I'm confident it's only the beginning of great and surprising business impacts. It's when the client's big move starts to pay off, signaling amazing results to come. That's the power of TV. That's the power of your team and our team coming together to build your brand and business.

For us, TV is more than a marketing tactic. We watch it unite great teams every day. And great teams can change the world.

Why not let TV help you do exactly that?

---

71 "TV Viewing Remains a Social Activity," Marketing Charts, January 24, 2019, https://www.marketingcharts.com/television/tv-audiences-and-consumption-107151.

Is Your Business Ready For Television?

IN THIS BOOK, YOU'VE LEARNED the impact TV advertising can have and how to approach it effectively. But how do you know whether TV can have that impact on your business specifically? We've created a survey using characteristics of brands that have found success on TV to help determine your TV readiness. For each question below, check all that apply.

① How would you describe your business?

☐ Our business model is working, and our people, systems, and processes are aligned.

☐ We have a proven growth assumption and measurable KPIs attached to marketing.

☐ We have optimized points of distribution (sales) and customer engagement.

☐ Our strategy and growth goals are clear, and we are tracking key milestones.

☐ We have a culture of making big moves and leveraging an "outside view" for ideas.

☐ We assign business value to marketing beyond immediate customer acquisition.

② Which of the following reflect your marketing capabilities?

☐ Our target market is clear, and all our marketing and sales efforts align with it.

☐ We have optimized search (paid, organic) and have effective retargeting in place.

☐ We monitor brand recall, know our aided and unaided scores, and understand impact to profit.

☐ We have optimized our sales funnel and prioritize ongoing testing.

☐ Our differentiators are clear, and we have clarified our messaging around them.

☐ We have an effective customer review system in place with high scores.

☐ We integrate our channels and deploy campaign concepts across all touchpoints.

③ Check all that reflect your marketing team.

☐ Our marketing team is in place, and they are performing at a high level.

☐ Our CEO is involved with marketing and has a high level of trust in the plan.

☐ Marketing is considered a function of everyone's job, and contributions are measured.

☐ We possess a strong sales culture and have resources to optimize consumer interest.

☐ Our analytics acumen crosses functions, and we balance judgment with science well.

☐ Our team has a process for productively debating and setting marketing strategy.

④ Which statements represent your advertising experience?

☐ We track our CPM for all paid channels and are getting strong ROI results.

☐ We have fully optimized our creative messaging and have identified the optimal creative refresh cadence.

☐ Our agency contacts are strategic and brief us regularly on opportunistic media and campaign performance through a dynamic system of engagement.

☐ We have clarity on our revenue contribution from our media mix and are confident our plan is fully optimized.

☐ Our sales funnel is optimized, and we work closely with our agency partner to integrate with our messaging and improve monetization.

☐ We regularly find big wins and align around bold campaign ideas derived by our agency from data insights that generate ever-increasing returns from our paid efforts.

☐ We have a long-term plan (three-plus years) in place that maps our paid media investment to business growth milestones, and we are tracking ahead of schedule.

☐ Our agency fee structure and overhead are providing value far beyond their cost, and the right incentives are in place to drive agency performance.

☐ We have full executive buy-in to our paid efforts, and we are clearly reaching major revenue milestones.

Once you've completed the survey, add up the number of boxes you checked. Match your total with the following results.

FOR SCORES LESS THAN 14:

It may be too early to test TV. However, we'd be happy to discuss how to get there.

FOR SCORES 14 TO 20:

You're almost there. TV could be a successful channel for your business in the future if approached carefully. Let's look at what key initiatives could help prepare your brand.

FOR SCORES GREATER THAN 20:

You're perfectly primed for success on TV. Let's get started!

ABOUT MARKETING ARCHITECTS

Marketing Architects is an All-Inclusive TV agency that gives performance brands access to quality, effective TV campaigns without the traditional high entry cost and ongoing optimization, scale, and measurement challenges. Founded in Minneapolis, Marketing Architects has been helping companies connect with their customers in new and surprising ways for more than twenty years. For more information, visit www.marketingarchitects.com.

CPSIA information can be obtained
at www.ICGtesting.com
Printed in the USA
BVHW080424070721
611240BV00013B/1685

9 781642 252828